God, Evil, and Morality

God, Evil, and Morality

A Debate

J. BRIAN HUFFLING
and GARY J. WHITTENBERGER

With
Michael Shermer,
James P. Sterba,
and Richard G. Howe

WIPF & STOCK · Eugene, Oregon

GOD, EVIL, AND MORALITY
A Debate

Copyright © 2024 J. Brian Huffling and Gary J. Whittenberger. All rights reserved. Except for brief quotations in critical publications or reviews, no part of this book may be reproduced in any manner without prior written permission from the publisher. Write: Permissions, Wipf and Stock Publishers, 199 W. 8th Ave., Suite 3, Eugene, OR 97401.

Wipf & Stock
An Imprint of Wipf and Stock Publishers
199 W. 8th Ave., Suite 3
Eugene, OR 97401

www.wipfandstock.com

PAPERBACK ISBN: 978-1-6667-8240-0
HARDCOVER ISBN: 978-1-6667-8241-7
EBOOK ISBN: 978-1-6667-8242-4

Cataloguing-in-Publication data:

Names: Huffling, J. Brian [author]. | Whittenberger, Gary J. [author]

Title: God, evil, and morality : a debate / by J. Brian Huffling and Gary J. Whittenberger, with Michael Shermer, James P. Sterba, and Richard G. Howe.

Description: Eugene, OR: Wipf and Stock, 2024 | Includes bibliographical references.

Identifiers: ISBN 978-1-6667-8240-0 (paperback) | ISBN 978-1-6667-8241-7 (hardcover) | ISBN 978-1-6667-8242-4 (ebook)

Subjects: LCSH: Theodicy. | Good and evil—Religious aspects. | Religion—Philosophy.

Classification: BL216 H84 2024 (paperback) | BL216 (ebook)

VERSION NUMBER 010224

Contents

Permissions | vii
Preface | ix
Contributors | xi
Introduction | xxv
   J. Brian Huffling

PART I: THE DEBATE

1. Evil and the Irrefutable God Problem | 3
   Michael Shermer

2. God Is Not a Moral Being | 11
   J. Brian Huffling

3. Harm and the Definition of God | 20
   Gary J. Whittenberger

4. Rejecting Divine Exceptionalism | 27
   J. Brian Huffling

5. God Is Not Huffgod | 34
   Gary J. Whittenberger

6. Rejecting the Standard Definition While Offering Arguments for God | 44
   J. Brian Huffling

7. Correct Universal Ethics and God's Moral Standing | 54
   Gary J. Whittenberger

8. God, Morality, and Aseity | 65
   J. Brian Huffling

9 Correct Universal Ethics and God's Transcendence | 75
   GARY J. WHITTENBERGER

10 God, Moral Propositions, and Truth | 89
   J. BRIAN HUFFLING

11 Summary | 103
   GARY J. WHITTENBERGER

12 Summary | 108
   J. BRIAN HUFFLING

PART II: COMMENTARIES ON THE DEBATE

13 Commentary from an Atheist | 115
   JAMES P. STERBA

14 Commentary from a Theist | 127
   RICHARD G. HOWE

Bibliography | 139

Permissions

Permission has been obtained for the following articles to be adapted for use as chapters:

Michael Shermer, "Is the Reality of Evil Good Evidence Against the Christian God? Notes from a Debate on the Problem of Evil." *Skeptic* 24.2 (2019) 42–48.

Brian Huffling, "Is the Reality of Evil Good Evidence Against the Christian God? A Response to Michael Shermer." *Skeptic* 24.2 (2019) 49–54.

Gary Whittenberger, "Does God Exist? A Rebuttal of Theologian Brian Huffling." *Skeptic* 24.4 (2019) 40–42.

Brian Huffling, "God is Not a Moral Being: A Response to Gary Whittenberger on the Problem of Evil." *Skeptic* 24.4 (2019) 43–45.

Scriptures taken from the Holy Bible, New International Version®, NIV®. Copyright © 1973, 1978, 1984, 2011 by Biblica, Inc.™ Used by permission of Zondervan. All rights reserved worldwide. www.zondervan.com The "NIV" and "New International Version" are trademarks registered in the United States Patent and Trademark Office by Biblica, Inc.™

Preface

This book started as an in-person debate between me (Brian Huffling) and Michael Shermer, which took place on February 23, 2019.[1] After our debate, Michael invited me to respond to an article he wrote in his magazine, *Skeptic* (he is the founding publisher). After our articles were published, Gary Whittenberger wrote a response to mine, and Michael invited me to respond to Gary. After our four articles were published, Gary and I continued conversing through email and decided to keep writing in the hopes of producing this book. We asked Michael if we could use the *Skeptic* articles as the first four chapters. Michael graciously agreed. Thus, the first four chapters are adaptations from the *Skeptic* articles. The first chapter is Michael's original article, with the second chapter being my response. The third chapter is Gary's initial response to me, with my response to him as the fourth chapter. The fifth through tenth chapters are a continuation of the debate between Gary and me. Chapters 11 and 12 are summaries of our positions. Chapters 13 and 14 are commentaries on the overall debate by James Sterba (atheist) and Richard Howe (theist).

These dialogues started off in a very informal way, and Gary and I agreed to keep the footnotes and references to a minimum as to lend the book to a more casual, conversational tone. We did not ask Richard and James to maintain such requirements.

1. https://brianhuffling.com/debates/, "If God, Why Evil?—A Debate on the Problem of Evil."

Contributors

MICHAEL SHERMER, PHD[2]

IN THESE PAGES YOU will find a spirited and open debate on the nature and problem of evil and the existence (or not) of God, between myself, Brian Huffling, and Gary J. Whittenberger. Its genesis, if you will, was February 23, 2019 when Dr. Huffling and I participated in a debate on this topic at Southern Evangelical Seminary in Charlotte, North Carolina. The debate was recorded and viewed by a sizable audience, which led to many letters and a brief print exchange between Dr. Huffling and me in the pages of *Skeptic* magazine, which I edit. That led to a print exchange between Huffling and Gary Whittenberger, a regular contributor to *Skeptic*, and then we all fine-tuned and expanded our positions that led to the book you hold in your hands.

The problem, put simply, goes like this:

- If God is all powerful, can he not prevent evil from existing?
- If God is all good, should he not prevent evil from existing?
- If evil exists, then either God is not all-powerful or not all-good.

As I argue in my opening statement within, I can think of several solutions to the problem, including:

---

2. Dr. Michael Shermer is the founding publisher of *Skeptic* magazine, the host of the podcast The Michael Shermer Show, and a presidential fellow at Chapman University where he teaches Skepticism 101. For eighteen years he was a monthly columnist for *Scientific American*. He writes a weekly Substack column. He is the author of *New York Times* bestsellers *Why People Believe Weird Things* and *The Believing Brain*, *Why Darwin Matters*, *The Science of Good and Evil*, *The Moral Arc*, *Heavens on Earth*, *Giving the Devil His Due: Reflections of a Scientific Humanist*, and *Conspiracy: Why the Rational Believe the Irrational*.

- God is all-powerful but is evil.
- God is all-good but not all-powerful so he cannot prevent evil.
- God is neither all-powerful nor all-good, so evil exists.

I won't keep you in suspense about my position, namely that there very probably is no God and bad things just happen and there's no one outside of us to do anything about it. But, if it were that simple you wouldn't need to read an entire book on the subject, so clearly theists like Brian Huffling have thoughtful arguments in response, in which they attempt to square that circle. Some of you will be convinced by Huffling, while others of you will be convinced by me and Whittenberger. It may ultimately be an insoluble problem, similar to the one over free will and determinism, which may explain why all of these issues have been debated by theologians, philosophers, and scientists for millennia.

My own introduction to these and related issues came when I became a born-again Christian in 1971 at the start of my senior year in high school. At the behest of my best friend George, I joined him and his family (including his beautiful sister Joyce, whom I was attracted to) at the Presbyterian church in Glendale, California, and at the end of the sermon when the preacher called people to come forward and be saved, I found myself inexplicably walking up the aisle with others to repeat the words from John 3:16: "For God so loved the world that he gave his one and only Son, that whoever believes in him shall not perish but have eternal life."

From that starting point at age seventeen, I became profoundly religious, fully embracing the belief that Jesus suffered wretchedly and died, not just for humanity, but for me personally. For me! It felt good. It seemed real. And for the next seven years I walked the talk. Literally. I went door-to-door and person-to-person, witnessing for God and evangelizing for Christianity. I became a "Bible thumper," as one of my friends called me, a "Jesus freak" in the words of a sibling. A little religion is one thing, but when it is all one talks about it can become awkward and uncomfortable for family and friends who don't share your faith passion.

I hung around other Christians at my high school, attended Bible-study classes, and participated in singing and socializing at a Christian house of worship called "The Barn" (literally a red house with barn-like features). I matriculated at Pepperdine University, a Church of Christ institution that mandated chapel attendance twice a week, along with a curriculum that included courses in the Old and New Testaments, the life of

Jesus, and the writings of C. S. Lewis. Although all this theological training would come in handy years later in my public debates on God, religion, and science, at the time I studied it because I believed it, and I believed it because I unquestioningly accepted God's existence as real, along with the resurrection of Jesus, and all the other tenets of the faith.

There were a number of factors involved in my de-conversion—in my becoming unborn, again—going back to my conversion experience. Shortly after I accepted Christ into my heart, I eagerly announced to my high school friend Frank that I had become a Christian. Expecting an enthusiastic embrace of acceptance into the club he had long cajoled me to join, Frank instead was disappointed that I had gone to a Presbyterian church—and *joined* no less!—which he explained was a big mistake because that was the "wrong" religion. Frank was a Jehovah's Witness.

After high school I attended Glendale College where my faith was tested by a number of secular professors, most notably Richard Hardison, whose philosophy course forced me to check my premises, along with my facts, which were not always sound or correct. But the Christian mantra was that when your belief is tested it is an opportunity for your faith in the Lord to grow. And grow it did, since there were some fairly serious challenges to my faith.

After Pepperdine, when I began my graduate studies in experimental psychology at the California State University, Fullerton, I was still a Christian, although the foundations of my faith were already cracking under the weight of other factors. Out of curiosity, I registered for an undergraduate course in evolutionary biology, which was taught by an irrepressible professor named Bayard Brattstrom, a herpetologist (one who studies amphibians and reptiles) and showman extraordinaire. The class met on Tuesday nights from 7:00 to 10:00 pm, during which I discovered that the evidence for evolution is undeniable and rich and the arguments for creationism that I had been reading were duplicitous and hollow. After Bayard exhausted himself with a three-hour display of erudition and entertainment, the class adjourned to the 301 Club in downtown Fullerton, a nightclub where students hung out to discuss The Big Questions, aided by adult beverages.

Although I had already been exposed to all sides in the great debates in my various courses and readings at Pepperdine, what was strikingly different in this context was the heterogeneity of my fellow students' beliefs. Since I was no longer exclusively surrounded by Christians there were no social penalties for being skeptical . . . about anything. Except for the 301

Club discussions that went on into the wee hours of the morning, however, religion almost never came up in the classroom or lab. We were there to do science, and that is almost all we did. Religion was simply not part of the environment.

There were other factors as well, and that brings me back to the problem of evil. My college sweetheart, Maureen Hannon, a brilliant and beautiful Alaskan whom I met at Pepperdine and whom I was still dating, was in a horrific automobile accident in the middle of the night in the middle of nowhere. Maureen worked for an inventory company that vanned their employees around the state during off hours, sleeping supine on bench seats between jobs. The van veered off the highway and rolled several times, snapping Maureen's back and rendering her paralyzed from the waist down.

When she called me in the wee hours of the morning from a Podunk hospital hours from Los Angeles, I figured it couldn't be too bad since she sounded as lucid and sanguine as ever. It wasn't until days later, after we had her transported to the Long Beach Medical Center to put her into their hyperbaric chamber to pressure-feed oxygen into her tissues to try to coax some life into her severely bruised spinal cord, that the full implications of what this meant for her begin to dawn on me. The cognizance of Maureen's prospects generated a sickening feeling in the pit of my stomach, an indescribable sense of dread—what's the point if it can all be taken away in the flash of a moment?

There, in the ER, day after dreary day, night after sleepless night, alternating between pacing up and down cold sterile hallways and sitting on hard plastic chairs in the waiting room listening to the moans and prayers of other grieving souls, I took a knee and bowed my head and asked God to heal Maureen's broken back. I prayed with deepest sincerity. I cried out to God to overlook my doubts in the name of Maureen. I willingly suspended all disbelief.

At that time and in that place, I was once again a believer. I believed because I wanted to believe that if there was any justice in the universe—any at all—this sweet, loving, smart, responsible, devoted, caring spirit did not deserve to be in a shattered body. A just and loving God who had the power to heal, would surely heal Maureen. He didn't.

He didn't, I now believe, not because "God works in mysterious ways" or "He has a special plan for Maureen"—the nauseatingly banal comforts believers sometimes offer in such trying and ultimately futile times—but because there very probably is no God.

J. BRIAN HUFFLING, PHD[3]

I WAS BROUGHT UP in a Christian home, went to church and Christian school, and became serious about my faith at the age of fourteen. I loved studying theology and towards the end of high school I decided to go to Lee University. I thought I wanted to be a pastor and started out majoring in pastoral studies but then changed to theology. I ultimately changed to history with a (required) minor in Bible. I wanted to be a professor since age nineteen, but close to college graduation I wanted to make sure I chose a profession that paid well. I thought I would become a lawyer. However, I could not shake my desire to learn theology, and I had my own questions about my faith. I didn't really doubt my faith, but I wanted to better understand why I thought Christianity was true. So, I enrolled in Southern Evangelical Seminary to major in Christian apologetics. I was privileged to study apologetics under folks like Norman Geisler, and Richard Howe, Tom Howe, and Barry Leventhal. In my first semester, I realized that I needed to study philosophy. I further thought I needed to learn the biblical languages. So, I ended up triple majoring in apologetics, philosophy, and biblical studies. I stayed at SES to attain a PhD in philosophy of religion.

When I started seminary, I was hired to work as a part-time youth pastor at a Korean church in Charlotte. I ended up working at four churches during my seminary time: two Korean and two American. Also, during my seminary days I joined the Chaplain Candidate program with the Air Force (having already served in the Marine and Naval reserves). I was ordained in a Southern Baptist church, where I was serving as associate pastor. I was endorsed by the Associated Gospel Churches. I have served as a chaplain

---

3. Dr. Brian Huffling is associate professor of philosophy and theology and the director of the PhD program at Southern Evangelical Seminary. He is a visiting scholar with Reasons to Believe. He has taught at The Art Institute of Charlotte, Arborbrook Christian Academy, and also teaches at Apologia. His BA is from Lee University in history with a minor in Bible. Brian has an MA in apologetics, philosophy, and biblical studies from Southern Evangelical Seminary. His PhD is in philosophy of religion from SES. He has authored various journal articles in the areas of philosophy, theology, and apologetics. Brian has engaged in several academic and popular-level debates. He has served on four church staffs. He has also served in the Marines and Navy reserves. He is currently a chaplain in the Air Force reserves.

at four bases: Seymour-Johnson Air Force Base, the Air Force Academy, Maxwell Air Force Base, and Dobbins Air Reserve Base.

The problem of evil is probably the most written about issue in Christian apologetics and perhaps in the philosophy of religion. For this reason, I didn't want anything to do with it. I did not want to write on it or have it as part of my research agenda. Further, I did not want to participate in debates on this topic. I was perfectly happy relegating the study to the MA and PhD classes I had on the issue. However, I was asked if I wanted to have a debate on God and evil with Michael Shermer. Finding this somewhat comical and ironic, I happily agreed. And I'm glad I did. I have enjoyed getting to know Michael and very much appreciate being able to interact with him in *Skeptic*, as well as here. I have also greatly enjoyed getting to know James Sterba. We have had two formal debates on this topic and two in-print discussions in *Religions*. He was also a guest lecturer in my class on the problem of evil, which I and my students enjoyed. I have known Richard for many years, and he has been one of my professors at SES. I greatly appreciate his willingness to add his commentary. I would especially like to thank Gary for both responding to my article in *Skeptic* as well as going back and forth with me to make this book. It has been nice getting to know him and working together.

At an apologetics conference a few years ago, I was asked, "What do you think is the most important apologetic issue for Christianity?" That didn't take much thought: the problem of evil. The reason is that everyone has experienced evil and suffering—no one is immune, and it is natural to ask why a good, all-powerful God would allow such things. Many come to the conclusions that evil is evidence against God while others see evil as somehow part of God's plan. I have seen many people experience all sorts of evil. I have also experienced evil and suffering. I have watched loved ones very close to me suffer and die. As a youth pastor I lost an eighteen year old to a drunk driver. One of my best friends was killed in the line of police duty. Such events have not caused me to question God's existence, but rather recognize that we don't have the answers. I have also watched families and friends of people who have suffered greatly, such as the family of my friend who was killed. Or the family of a good friend of mine who lost their brother as a victim of a gang initiation. A childhood friend and his wife lost a three year old during the night. Rather than rejecting God, these people who suffered greatly were drawn even closer to God. The family of my friend showed great courage and reached out for God rather than shunning him. His father even called on us to forgive the person who shot his son. I have two friends who are paraplegics who love God. I am legally blind in one eye. The evil around us does not invalidate good reasons for God's existence or brush away the miraculous life of Jesus. Rather than evil being an objection to Christianity, without evil, there would be no Christianity. Christianity helps us to make sense of evil. Atheism offers no answer.

GARY J. WHITTENBERGER, PHD[4]

I AM HAPPY TO have been a co-author with Brian Huffling and Michael Shermer in writing this book—*God, Evil, and Morality: A Debate*. I am also grateful to our commentators, James Sterba and Richard Howe, who have offered useful perspectives. As Michael has alluded to, I have been a regular reader and contributor to *Skeptic* magazine of which Michael is the editor. In the Vol. 24, No. 2, 2019 issue of the magazine I read an exchange in views on God and the "problem of evil" between Michael and Brian, and I was immediately intrigued by and very irritated with Brian's presentation. Both Brian and I negotiated with Michael for publication of an additional exchange of our views on the same topic in *Skeptic*. Brian and I elaborated on our positions in the Vol. 24, No. 4, 2019 issue of the magazine. Thereafter, Brian and I continued our debate by email and finally we agreed to work on a book which we have now been able to publish. Although Brian and I have disagreed greatly, I have much appreciated his civility and cooperation.

    I grew up in a town in northern Indiana, population approximately one thousand. During our elementary school years my brother and I were sent by my mother to Sunday school at one of the three local Protestant churches, specifically the one in the Church of God denomination. My religious indoctrination progressed rapidly, and by high school I was a devout Christian. I was "saved" through altar calls two or three times. I attended church camp. I even cajoled my brother into our attempt to memorize Genesis. I read the Bible from cover to cover, the King James Version, of course.

---

4. Dr. Gary Whittenberger PhD is a freelance writer and retired psychologist, living in North Hollywood, California. He received his doctoral degree from Florida State University after which he worked for twenty-three years as a psychologist in prisons. He has written many published articles on science, philosophy, psychology, and religion, and he is a member of several freethought organizations. He is the author of two books: *God Wants You to Be an Atheist: The Startling Conclusion from a Rational Analysis* and *God and Natural Disasters: A Debate between an Atheist and a Christian.*

For a short while I made plans to study for the ministry. However, in the summer of 1967 I finally decided to major in psychology at the university.

I attended Purdue University in West Lafayette, Indiana. This university was well known for engineering, the physical sciences, and agriculture, and I believe it has produced more astronauts than any other university in the world. Here a student majoring in psychology was like a step-child. By many of my peers psychology was considered a "soft science" or not a science at all. Nevertheless, I persevered. I was exposed to many new ideas—Big Bang cosmology, evolution, calculus, and the possibility that religions were man-made. I minored in philosophy, which had always held my interest. It was my good fortune to take a class from professor William L. Rowe, in which I had my first exposure to the "problem of evil." Later on, I learned that Dr. Rowe had published some of the most illuminating and reputable papers in the philosophy of religion about "the problem." On my visits home I began to disagree with my parents about religion and politics. My dad and I had heated arguments about the Vietnam War. He was a WWII veteran, and he favored the war to stop communism, while I opposed the war. My attitudes, values, and worldview were changing. Over the course of my sophomore year at Purdue, I converted from fundamentalist Christian to deist to agnostic to atheist and secular humanist. These were pretty profound changes for a small town kid from Indiana.

After graduating from Purdue, I took a year off from school, worked in a factory and stashed away some money for my next phase of life, applied to graduate schools, and got married to a woman who had been my middle-school sweetheart. Life looked bright for me, especially when I was accepted to graduate school at Florida State University (FSU). Then my life took a drastic turn for the worse. After only eight months of marriage, my wife was killed in an automobile accident. Why? Why did this happen to me? I was forced to confront the "problem of evil" again, this time in a very personal way. I went through a period of grief and depression. I read the Bible again from cover to cover, searching for answers. In the end I remained an atheist. If God did exist, then he would not have caused or allowed the premature death of my wife. But she died in a horrible accident. Thus, God did not exist. I was now sure of it.

I studied clinical psychology at FSU, acquired my masters and doctoral degrees, and then took a job with the federal prison system. I got married for the second time and we had a child. I retired after twenty-five years of work mostly in correctional psychology, particularly in the development, management, and oversight of substance-abuse treatment programs for inmates. After my retirement from clinical and correctional psychology, I devoted myself to writing, particularly in the areas of philosophy, religion, social issues, and skepticism.

During my life I have experienced various difficulties and tragedies, including the deaths of my parents and a few close friends, a severely broken ankle with months of recovery, the two-month premature delivery of my granddaughter, five instances of breast and kidney cancer suffered by my second wife, and her death from brain and liver disorders after we had been married for forty-five years. Through all of these life experiences I became stronger in my belief that God does not exist.

Like Michael, I am an atheist, but my position is stronger than his. He believes that "God probably does not exist," whereas I have come to *know* that God does not exist. What does it mean to "know" something? According to the most accepted epistemological framework, knowledge is "justified true belief." I strongly believe that God does not exist, and this belief is true and justified! Therefore, I *know* that God does not exist. Over about the last five years, I have been developing various proofs that God does not exist. It can be rationally and conclusively demonstrated that the existence of God is incompatible with what we know about reality and the universe. I have been influenced in my studies by Bertrand Russell, Sam Harris, Richard Dawkins, Daniel Dennett, Christopher Hitchens, Bart Ehrman, Sean Carroll, Victor Stenger, Harry Kroto, Richard Hull, Harold Hawkins, and more recently by James Sterba. Today I proudly stand as a secular humanist, skeptic, rationalist, naturalist, progressive, agnostic, and atheist.

JAMES P. STERBA, PHD[5]

While I defend atheism in my commentary on Shermer's, Huffling's, and Whittenberger's, work, I have not always been an atheist. In fact, I was in a religious order for twelve years leaving only just before I would have had

---

5. Dr. James P. Sterba teaches graduate and undergraduate courses in ethics and political philosophy at Notre Dame. He has published thirty-five books, and over two hundred articles. And he is past president of the American Philosophical Association, Central Division, the North American Society for Social Philosophy, past president of Concerned Philosophers for Peace, and past president of the International Association for Philosophy of Law and Social Philosophy, American Section. He has been visiting professor of philosophy at the University of Rochester and at the University of Latvia in the then Soviet Union on a Fulbright Award.

to have taken final vows at age twenty-six. And I only became an atheist recently after accepting a John Templeton grant to apply the yet untapped resources of ethics and political philosophy to the problem of evil. Work on this Templeton grant ultimately resulted in my developing an argument that the all-good, all-powerful God of traditional theism is logically incompatible with all the evil in the world. I have summarized this argument in my commentary on Shermer's, Huffling's, and Whittenberger's, work, and have set it out in more detail in my book *Is a Good God Logically Possible?* (Palgrave/Macmillan, 2019). Moreover, if anyone is successful in poking a hole in my argument, I am happy to give up being an atheist. My commitment to atheism is only as strong as the soundness and validity of my argument. Undercut my argument and poof, at least in my case, no more atheist.

RICHARD G. HOWE, PHD[6]

Being a professor of philosophy and Christian apologetics affords me many opportunities to engage with issues (both in speaking and writing) regarding the truth of major Christian doctrines with fellow Christians and with non-Christians. Such issues include the existence and attributes of God—Michael and I once debated the existence of God in Colorado Springs in April of 2010—and the topic before us: the problem of evil. Perhaps a few facts about my experience that led me to this way of life are in order.

I was reared with four brothers in a very loving, stable, middle-class, suburban, southern U.S. home in what is sometimes disparagingly referred to as the "Bible Belt"—Mississippi to be exact. Despite that, and perhaps against the odds, our home was devoid of any outward religious faith. Our parents were loving and hard-working. While my mom was a nominal Christian, my dad was an atheist. He was never hostile to religion, but because of his unbelief, church was never a part of the family routine. As such, I can remember never hearing the name of Jesus from anyone until very close to my teenage years. Despite this, as far back as my memory goes as a young child, I always believed in the existence of God. That belief was never challenged. God's existence seemed so obvious to me, I never even challenged myself.

---

6. Dr. Richard G. Howe is provost, Norman L. Geisler Chair of Christian Apologetics, and professor of philosophy and apologetics at Southern Evangelical Seminary. He has a BA in Bible from Mississippi College, an MA in philosophy from the University of Mississippi, and a PhD in philosophy from the University of Arkansas.

I began to become concerned with the specifics of Christianity around fourteen years old. Being too young to drive, I remember having my mom drop me off at church. I chose to attend the same church as my friends did. More because of personal fears rather than moral conviction, I avoided the common traps of alcohol or drugs into which youth often fall. This moved me to avoid those classmates whom I would soon encounter who were involved in such activities. Perhaps not surprisingly, those around me who were rather chaste, were so because of their own Christian commitment. These where the ones with whom I wanted to be friends. Through their influence, I began to learn and understand the Christian gospel. These experiences culminated in me becoming a Christian at the age of sixteen.

I grew in my Christian faith about as much and as fast as one might expect a teenager to grow. After high school, I headed to college. Having no real clarity as to what direction I wanted my life to head, I followed the footsteps of my best friend by majoring in music at the nearby community college. I had been a garage-band type of drummer for several years. Music seemed as good a choice—perhaps better in many ways—as anything else. But it did not take long for me to discover that music was not a career path for me. That is when I learned that one could go to college and study the Bible. That was the most remarkable thing I had ever heard. Because I loved studying the Bible, I immediately aimed in that direction, transferring to the flagship Christian denominational liberal arts college in my state.

This is where the questions of Christian apologetics became relevant. Perhaps ironically to some (but not surprising to those familiar with contemporary "Christian" academics), I was confronted with the first major challenges to my Christianity as a Bible major. These initial challenges involved issues relating to both the textual and theological integrity of the Bible. All of my professors were professing Christians, but few of them believed in biblical inerrancy. The doubts about Christianity grew to the point where I was no longer sure what to believe about Jesus.

Suffice it to say, I struggled with my convictions for several years in confrontations with fellow students as well as with my two oldest brothers who, by this time, had become Christians relatively independently of me. Some of my fellow students went on to renounce their Christianity, mockingly asking Jesus to "come out of their hearts." Others settled for a liberal form of Christianity. Still others seemingly amputated their intellects, deciding to shelve such debates as irrelevant to the Christian life. None of these options would work for me. I could not ignore the questions. I could not live with the intellectual dissonance. Either full-on Christianity was true or it was not. In reading numerous resources on the subject of biblical inerrancy, I eventually came back to a firm conviction.

Admittedly, many Christians today deny biblical inerrancy. Certain luminaries from Christian history, C. S. Lewis, for example, denied biblical inerrancy. Though convinced of the truth of inerrancy and its importance for the Christian, both personally and academically, I acknowledge that someone can be a Christian even while denying biblical inerrancy. But as interesting as this might seem, it still does not fully engage the issue before us in this book. Many thinkers throughout history regard the problem of evil as insurmountable for any Christian notion of God. How did the question of God's existence fare for me over the years?

During those years of intellectual struggle, I never wavered in my conviction of God's existence. Having intellectually regained my faith and having developed a desire for some sort of "ministry" (though definitely not in the pulpit), I assumed the next step after my BA was seminary. This led me to become a disciple of Norman L. Geisler at Dallas Theological Seminary. As excited and honored as I felt to be there, something was missing. Some itch was not being scratched. I wasn't sure how to engage my interests in apologetics.

Then, Geisler gave me the best advice I could have received at the time. He suggested that I interrupt my seminary studies and return to the university to study philosophy. He knew then what I came to understand later that, although not every apologetic issue is philosophical, many are directly so, including the existence and attributes of God and the problem of evil.

While I had encountered some philosophy during my BA and in my apologetics studies with Geisler, I had no thorough training. My foray into graduate academic philosophy was with Alfred North Whitehead and Ludwig Wittgenstein. Any philosopher reading this will understand how challenging that can be. No doubt Michael would consider such an endeavor as this as just so much "philosophical jargon" designed to obfuscate any debate. I have found it to be very much the opposite. This is not to say that every philosopher has something to say about the existence and attributes of God and the problem of evil. But it cannot be denied that the problem of evil, intellectually (as opposed to pastorally) speaking, is very much philosophical.

Having completed the MA in philosophy at Ole Miss, I eventually completed the PhD in philosophy at the University of Arkansas. One should note that these are both state universities. I did not confine my philosophical studies to an intellectually sheltered environment. Some of my professors were professing Christians. Some were not. All of them enriched my life by confronting me with the thinking of the great philosophers of history. It was up to me to engage the ideas in the context of my Christianity. I must say with all sincerity, my conviction of the existence of the God of classical Christianity, including the conviction that God is good, has only grown with my studies. Today God's existence and attributes have become the focus of much of my philosophical and apologetical life.

Am I saying that no idea I ever encountered gave me pause regarding anything about God? No, I am not saying this. At the fear of sounding facetious, I vividly remember one day after a logic class wondering for about ninety seconds how I could reconcile God's omniscience with the notions of sets and supersets. My view of God would not let me retain God's existence and abandon omniscience. Just as quickly as the doubt arose in my mind, it melted away as I pondered the issue while walking across campus. One should note that it was never the problem of evil that gave rise to any reconsideration of God's existence or, for that matter, God's goodness. This is because these issues are decidedly metaphysical issues that can be demonstrated by sound philosophy. As I see it, it is not a question of induction or any "argument to the best explanation" as it is often framed. The specifics of this are readily available to anyone who is interested. For my purposes here, I will leave it to the reader to seek out and consider.

Introduction

J. Brian Huffling

The problem of evil goes back to ancient times. Usually, it is first credited to Epicurus.[7] The problem can be formulated in several ways and has many aspects. One aspect is the emotional or pastoral concern about evil, which asks, "Why does God allow evil and suffering?" The problem understood in this way does not question God's existence. The intellectual problem of evil, however, does question God's existence. It is the latter formulation that this book is about. While the pastoral or emotional problem is certainly important, that is an issue that is not dealt with here. The purpose of this book is to debate whether God can exist in the face of so much evil.

From an atheistic point of view, the problem serves to show the impossibility, or at least the improbability, of God's existence. Atheists disagree as to how successful the various arguments are for such a reason. For theists, the problem is one to be overcome if theism is to be maintained. It is likely the case that the problem of evil is the strongest and most used argument against theism.

WHAT IS "EVIL"

While not everyone agrees on the nature of evil, there is a general consensus in the literature and in everyday life as to what it is.[8] Philosophers have often distinguished natural and moral evil. Natural evil would be the harm

---

7. Although, as Howe notes in his commentary, it is questioned as to whether or not Epicurus actually is responsible for it.

8. In this text, Whittenberger objects to the notion of evil in terms of what he considers outdated religious or theological notions. He would prefer that the concept of harm replace the concept of evil in these types of discussions.

caused by something that comes about naturally without a human agent intentionally causing it. For that reason, it does not have an obvious moral component (e.g., cancer, tornadoes, and hurricanes). Moral evil would be intentional harm by a rational being (e.g., murder). Theistic philosophers and theologians have traditionally held, following Augustine, that evil is a privation or corruption of something that is good. A typical example has been the eye. The eye is supposed to have all its parts to be able to see, but if there is something wrong with the eye and it cannot see, then according to this understanding of evil, there would be a privation of a good (sight) that is supposed to be there. Trees and rocks don't have sight, but since they are not supposed to, they do not have such a privation or evil. Such privations could be physical in nature, such as the damaged eye or a lost limb, or moral in terms of a person being corrupted in his nature or lacking virtue that he should have.[9]

TYPES OF THE PROBLEM OF EVIL

The problem of evil comes in two basic forms: the logical, which is also called the deductive form, and the evidential, which is also called the inductive form. The logical problem argues that there is no logical possibility that God can exist given evil. Such was the argument of David Hume, J. L. Mackie, and more recently James Sterba.[10] This is the style of the problem that Shermer, Whittenberger, and Sterba use in this book. This form of the argument normally looks like this:

1. If an all-powerful, all-knowing, all-good God exists, then evil wouldn't exist.

2. Evil exists.

3. Therefore, an all-powerful, all-knowing, all-good God does not exist.

---

9. For such a view of evil, see Augustine, *Confessions* III, 7, §12 and Aquinas, *Summa Contra Gentiles*, III, 7, §2.

10. See Hume's *Dialogues*, 84; Mackie, "Evil and Omnipotence," 200–201; and Sterba, *Is a Good God*. I should clarify that while Shermer used the logical argument in his opening remarks (from the *Stanford Encyclopedia*) he did not seem to hold the strong conclusion that God *cannot* exist. He's more of an agnostic. It should be also noted that Mackie gave up the logical problem due to his debates with Alvin Plantinga. See Mackie, *Miracle*, 84. See below for a discussion on that.

Given the logical form, the conclusion necessarily follows from the premises, so if the premises are true, then so is the conclusion. This type of the argument leaves no room for the simultaneous existence of the God of theism and evil.

The evidential problem, on the other hand, is not as ambitious as the logical problem in that it simply argues that God *probably* does not exist (not that there is no logical way he can coexist with evil). William Rowe has become the champion of such a view.[11] For example, where E1 and E2 stand for particular evils, he argues, "P: No good we know of justifies an omnipotent, omniscient, perfectly good being in permitting E1 and E2; therefore, Q: no good at all justifies an omnipotent, omniscient, perfectly good being in permitting E1 and E2; therefore, not-G: there is no omnipotent, omniscient, perfectly good being."[12] Here he states, "The first inference, from P to Q, is, of course, an inductive inference."[13] In other words, there is no logical guarantee against God, but God likely doesn't exist given the amount of evil in the world.

RESPONSES TO THE PROBLEM OF EVIL

Theists have various responses to the above statements of the problem of evil. They generally fall into one of two categories: theodicies and defenses. A theodicy is an attempt to explain *why* God allows evil, whereas a defense is an explanation for *how* God can exist alongside evil. Theodicies are generally seen as more ambitious as they claim to know the motivations God has for allowing evil. Defenses do not claim to know why God allows evil but merely offer a logical account for why there is no contradiction in God doing so.

One popular example of a theodicy is John Hick's soul-making theodicy. Hick argues that God allows his creatures to undergo evil and suffering to help them grow as people and "become children of God through their

---

11. See Rowe's, "Varieties" and "Evidential Argument," both in Howard-Snyder, *The Evidential Argument*.

12. Rowe, "Evidential Argument," 263 in Howard-Snyder, *The Evidential Argument*.

13. Rowe, "Evidential Argument," 263 in Howard-Snyder, *The Evidential Argument*. It should be noted that Rowe in the cited essay claims that such is "at best, a weak argument" and that he proposes "to abandon this argument altogether" (267) and provide a better one which goes straight from Q to not-G (270).

own moral and spiritual choices," which can only happen in the kind of world we live in.[14]

Another type of theodicy is the so-called "greater good" theodicy. As with all theodicies, there are variations on how they are argued; however, in general, the greater good theodicy maintains that evil is allowed to serve the possibility of a greater good that would not be had without it. For example, courage could not be had without fear. Forgiveness could not happen without an offense. Thus, for these goods to be possible, there must be evil.[15]

Similar to a greater good theodicy is the best of all possible worlds argument. Championed by Leibniz, the argument here is that this is the best of all possible worlds that God could have made. This usually assumes that God, as a moral agent, is under some obligation to make the best possible world, since perfect beings would only bring about either perfect or as perfect as possible effects. Given that we are in this world and that God is said to be perfect, this must be the best possible world that God could have made.[16]

Probably the most popular defense is the free will defense set forth in recent times by Alvin Plantinga. In short, Plantinga argues that it is not logically possible for God to give creatures free will without also allowing the possibility for them causing evil. Since free will is a good worth having, according to Plantinga, the possibility of evil cannot be avoided.[17] The free-will defense is largely aimed at J. L. Mackie, and it was instrumental in Mackie admitting that the logical problem is now defeated.[18]

Another defense is known as skeptical theism. The thrust of skeptical theism is that, given our incredibly limited knowledge of reality, let alone God, we don't really understand the nature of the goods and evils that are possible, to say nothing of the fact that we don't know what reasons God may have for allowing such evils. This view maintains that there may well be good reasons for evil, but we have no access to them.[19] As Stephen Wykstra asserts, "What unites all versions, as I see it, is a twofold claim. First, there

---

14. Hick, "Soul-Making Theodicy," 273 in Peterson, *The Problem of Evil*.

15. For one example of such type of an argument, see Augustine, "A Good Creation's Capacity for Evil," in Peterson, *Problem of Evil*.

16. See Leibniz, *Theodicy*.

17. Plantinga, *God, Freedom, and Evil*, chapter 4.

18. Mackie, *Miracle of Theism*, 84.

19. See Bergmann, "Skeptical Theism," chapter 19 in Peterson, *The Problem of Evil*.

is the claim that *if* the God of theism exists, we humans should not expect to see or grasp very much of God's purposes for divine actions—including the divine actions of allowing or even causing events that bring much of the horrific suffering around us. Second, there is the claim that if the first claim is true, then much of what otherwise looks like strong evidence against theism isn't very strong at all."[20]

A different way of dealing with the problem of evil is to argue that God does not need justifying or defending since God has no moral obligations, and that therefore no such problem of evil exists as it relates to God's existence. According to this view, those who maintain there is a real problem of evil, atheists and theists alike, take God to be a moral being with obligations to prevent such evils, at least horrendous evils.[21] This non-moral view is based on a position that is attributed to the overall metaphysics of Aristotle and Thomas Aquinas as interpreted by Herbert McCabe and Brian Davies.[22] It is represented by Brian Huffling in this book. According to such thinking, if there are good reasons and arguments for God's existence, then evil could not negate those. Further, if God is a necessary being (i.e., must exist), then evil could not even in principle be an argument against God. Such arguments for God being necessary can be seen in the writings of Aquinas.[23]

This introduction is certainly not meant to be exhaustive or even detailed. It serves as a basic overview for readers who are new to the subject, so they are more aware of the issues prior to reading the text of this book. Readers who wish to examine these topics further are encouraged to examine the texts referred to in the citations and bibliography. It is our sincere hope that readers will benefit from this work and that this will further the conversation on these topics.

In chapter 1, Shermer lays out the basic argument against God due to the amount of evil in the world by explaining the debate with Huffling at Southern Evangelical Seminary. In chapter 2, Huffling argues that the debate about God, contra Shermer, is not a scientific argument; rather, it is inherently philosophical. Huffling discusses the nature of science and

---

20. Wykstra, "A Skeptical Theist View," 99–100.

21. Horrendous evils are usually defined as those evils that would make a life not worth living. See Adams, *Horrendous Evils*.

22. See McCabe, *God and Evil* and Davies, *The Reality of God*.

23. For the five ways of Aquinas see his *Summa Theologica*, I, q. 2. a. 3. Other arguments for God being a cause of the universe would include the kalam. See Craig's, *Kalām*.

philosophy, including evil. The main point of the chapter is to argue that God is not a moral being, which, if true, would deflate a premise of the argument from evil. Chapter 3 is a response from Whittenberger which provides various arguments from evil (he prefers the term "harm") in an attempt to show God doesn't exist. He pulls from Shermer's chapter while also trying to demonstrate, *contra* Huffling, that if God exists and were a rational being, then he would be a moral agent and thus obliged to prevent harm. In chapter 4, Huffling addresses the material Whittenberger presented for God being moral as well as the charge of committing what Whittenberger calls "divine exceptionalism," among other issues, such as the nature of science, and other scientific arguments against God, such as arguments about petitionary prayer. Huffling attempts to provide more philosophical reasoning for his argument that God is not a moral being and that Whittenberger is simply begging the question by defining God a certain way. The main thrust of chapter 5 is Whittenberger's argument to describe the nature of what God would be like if he existed. At this point Whittenberger makes a distinction between the way Huffling describes God (primarily as non-moral), calling that view of God "Huffgod." It is Whittenberger's attempt to demonstrate that God as a rational being would be moral and that Huffling's argument is flawed in various ways. In chapter 6, Huffling rejects the standard definition that Whittenberger argues for, and retorts that we cannot merely define God in a certain way. Huffling explores several problems with the standard definition that Whittenberger maintains and provides various arguments for God's existence and nature. It is argued that if God exists, the problem of evil does not nullify his existence. In chapter 7, Whittenberger argues against the theistic proofs Huffling presented in chapter 6. He also provides the reason for why he believes God is a moral being, namely by creating and adhering to what he calls "Correct Universal Ethics" (CUE). Much of his arguments have to do with stipulating that God is indeed a moral being with moral obligations. To this point he attempts to refute Huffling's various arguments that God is not. In chapter 8, Huffling responds to much of what Whittenberger says in chapter 7, in part by revisiting an argument Huffling made in a previous chapter that attempts to demonstrate that God is not moral. Huffling argues that there is a contradiction between CUE and divine aseity (the doctrine that God is completely independent from everything and doesn't rely on anything, which is discussed in chapter 6). If divine aseity can be rejected, Huffling wants to know why divine morality can't be. Chapter 9 primarily focuses on CUE, divine aseity, and how the two relate while trying to make sense of God's transcendence (if he exists). Whittenberger attempts to demonstrate how CUE accounts for God's morality. He argues against Huffling's views of divine aseity and what that would mean for CUE and God's moral nature. In chapter 10, Huffling addresses the responses Whittenberger gives to his argument that moral properties are properties of creation. Huffling says that if moral propositions have no truth value (a claim Whittenberger made in chapter 9), then Whittenberger's arguments are unsound by definition since Whittenberger's arguments are comprised of moral propositions and as such, the problem of evil (harm) as Whittenberger constructs it, fails. Chapters 11 and 12 are summary chapters; although, in Whittenberger's summary he addresses the arguments Huffling made in chapter 10 about propositions and how and if they relate to God. Chapter 13 is an analysis of the overall debate by James Sterba. Not only does he critique all three in the debate, he offers his own solution to the problem of evil by arguing that there are no scenarios in which an omnipotent being needed to allow horrendous evils in order to secure the goods that many theists argue can only be had with such evil. In chapter 14, Richard Howe critiques the debate and leans on a moderate realist philosophy and classical theism to argue that Shermer and Whittenberger's views are faulty.

PART I

The Debate

1

Evil and the Irrefutable God Problem[1]

Michael Shermer

What is the problem of evil? As outlined in the *Stanford Encyclopedia of Philosophy*[2]:

1. If God exists, then God is omnipotent, omniscient, and morally perfect.
2. If God is omnipotent, then God has the power to eliminate all evil.
3. If God is omniscient, then God knows when evil exists.
4. If God is morally perfect, then God has the desire to eliminate all evil.
5. Evil exists.
6. If evil exists and God exists, then either God doesn't have the power to eliminate all evil, or doesn't know when evil exists, or doesn't have the desire to eliminate all evil.
7. Therefore, God doesn't exist. In brief, the following three conditions are incompatible:
1. God is Omnipotent (all powerful)
2. God is Omnibenevolent (all good)
3. Evil Exists

---

1. This chapter is adapted from Shermer, "Reality of Evil."
2. Tooley, "Evil," in *Stanford Encyclopedia of Philosophy*.

That is:

1. If God is all powerful, can he not prevent evil from existing?
2. If God is all good, should he not prevent evil from existing?
3. If evil exists, then either God is not all powerful or not all good.

The problem of evil is as old as philosophy itself, first articulated by Epicurus in around 300 BCE:

- Is God willing to prevent evil, but not able? Then he is not omnipotent.
- Is he able, but not willing? Then he is malevolent.
- Is he both able and willing? Then whence cometh evil?
- Is he neither able nor willing? Then why call him God?

Several solutions to the problem of evil come to mind:

1. God is all powerful but is evil.
2. God is all good but not all powerful so he cannot prevent evil.
3. God is neither all powerful nor all good, so evil exists.

My solution to this problem is simple: There is no God!

I agree with the *Oxford Companion to Philosophy*, which concludes that the problem of how a good and loving God can allow evil to afflict its creations "has always been the most powerful objection to traditional theism." Let's consider examples of evil. According to UNICEF, about 29,000 children under the age of five die every day, mainly from preventable causes. That's twenty-one dead children each minute, 10.6 million a year, the equivalent of the Holocaust (including non-Jewish victims).

More than 70 percent of the 10.6 million child deaths every year are attributable to six causes: diarrhea, malaria, neonatal infection, pneumonia, preterm delivery, or lack of oxygen at birth.

Science's response to this evil is that these are all preventable deaths, and people like Bill Gates are using the best science, technology, and medicine to do just that.

Religion's response to this evil is that these are all part of "God's plan."

Really? What sort of God would make a plan like this? An all-powerful, all-good god? Or a less than powerful, not so good god? Or no god at all?

The belief that what these children need is salvation from Jesus is somewhere between absurd and obscene. What these children need is potable water, vitamins, vaccinations, mosquito nets, antibacterial drugs, toilets, sanitation systems, etc., not Jesus.

The problem of evil for Christians is what I call the "irrefutable God problem":

1. When good things happen, who gets the credit? God.
2. When bad things happen, who gets the blame? Not God!

So . . . no matter what happens, the God hypothesis is confirmed. What would disconfirm the God hypothesis? Good things happen so God is. Bad things happen so God is. What would have to happen to refute this causal explanation of evil? In the Christian worldview, nothing can refute it. It is irrefutable—true by assertion, and as Christopher Hitchens said, "that which can be asserted without evidence can be dismissed without evidence." My friend Sam Harris has articulated the inanity of such beliefs when put into context. For example, "If you believe that your granola is the body of Christ and the milk is his blood . . . you're insane. But if you think a cracker is the body of Christ and the wine is his blood . . . you're just a Catholic."

Similarly, and with more dire consequences, if you claim to talk to God and he told you to go invade Afghanistan and Iraq, you're the president of the United States, George W. Bush. But if you were the president and you claimed to talk to God through your hairdryer, a national emergency would be declared. I fail to see how the addition of a hairdryer makes the claim more ridiculous or offensive.

Here I insert what I call Sagan's dragon, a thought experiment Carl Sagan presents in his 1996 book *The Demon-Haunted World* to illustrate the necessity of falsifiability in order to attain reliable knowledge (an example Sagan attributes to the psychologist Richard Franklin). I usually just tell the story in my own words, but here I will allow Carl to articulate the argument:

> "A fire-breathing dragon lives in my garage." Suppose I seriously make such an assertion to you. Surely, you'd want to check it out, see for yourself. There have been innumerable stories of dragons over the centuries, but no real evidence. What an opportunity! "Show me," you say. I lead you to my garage. You look inside and see a ladder, empty paint cans, an old tricycle—but no dragon. "Where's the dragon?" you ask. "Oh, she's right here," I reply, waving vaguely. "I neglected to mention that she's an invisible dragon."

You propose spreading flour on the floor of the garage to capture the dragon's footprints. "Good idea," I say, "but this dragon floats in the air." Then you'll use an infrared sensor to detect the invisible fire. "Good idea, but the invisible fire is also heatless." You'll spray-paint the dragon and make her visible. "Good idea, but she's an incorporeal dragon and the paint won't stick." And so on. I counter every physical test you propose with a special explanation of why it won't work.

Now, what's the difference between an invisible, incorporeal, floating dragon who spits heatless fire and no dragon at all? If there's no way to disprove my contention, no conceivable experiment that would count against it, what does it mean to say that my dragon exists?

Your inability to invalidate my hypothesis is not at all the same thing as proving it true. Claims that cannot be tested, assertions immune to disproof are veridically worthless, whatever value they may have in inspiring us or in exciting our sense of wonder. What I'm asking you to do comes down to believing, in the absence of evidence, on my say-so.

The analogy with the "irrefutable God problem" is clear: What's the difference between an invisible and irrefutable God and a nonexistent God? None! Arguing along these lines is like playing baseball—without the bases . . . or the ball.

The problem of evil is related to what I call the witch theory of causality: If your theory of evil is that your neighbor cavorts with the devil at night, flies around on a broom inflicting people, crops, and cattle with disease, and that the proper way to cure the problem of evil is to burn her at the stake, then you are either insane or you lived in Christian Europe 400 years ago when nearly everyone believed this. Worse, people act on their beliefs, mistaken as they may be, and this (in part) is why we end up with genocides, such as the witch crazes that afflicted Europe for centuries. As I explained the logic in my 2015 book *The Moral Arc*:

> If you-and everyone around you, including ecclesiastical and political authorities, truly believe that witches cause disease, crop failures, sickness, catastrophes, and accidents, then it is not only a rational act to burn witches, it is a moral duty. This is what Voltaire meant when he wrote that people who believe absurdities are more likely to commit atrocities. An even more pertinent translation of his famous quote is relevant here: "Truly, whoever is able to make you absurd is able to make you unjust."

The problem can be explained by a famous thought experiment that reveals the underlying logic behind such barbarous acts:

> Consider a popular thought experiment and how you would respond in the following scenario: You are standing next to a fork in a railroad line and a switch to divert a trolley car that is about to kill five workers on the track unless you throw the switch and divert the trolley down a side track where it will kill one worker. Would you throw the switch to kill one but save five? Most people say that they would. We should not be surprised, then, that our medieval ancestors performed the same kind of moral calculation in the case of witches. Medieval witch-burners torched women primarily out of a utilitarian calculus—better to kill the few to save the many. Other motives were present as well, of course, including scapegoating, the settling of personal scores, revenge against enemies, property confiscation, the elimination of marginalized and powerless people, and misogyny and gender politics. But these were secondary incentives grafted on to a system already in place that was based on a faulty understanding of causality.

This Christian theory of evil, in fact, is grounded in scripture, to wit Exodus 22:18: "Do not allow a [witch] to live." Today, no one in their right mind believes this. Why? Because science debunked the witch theory of evil. As I explained in *The Moral Arc*:

> We know that crops can fail due to disease, which we study through the science of agronomy and the etiology of disease; or they fail due to insects that we can investigate through the science of entomology and further control through chemistry; or they fail due to inclement weather that we can understand through the science of meteorology. Ecologists and biologists can tell us why populations of fish rise and fall and what we can do to prevent a region being fished out or decimated by disease or climate change. Psychologists specializing in marital counseling can explain why a wife might not be as responsive as her husband may wish (and vice versa); and though there may not be a big call for this sort of thing these days, psychologists who study personality and temperament could explain why some princes are cold and distant while others are warm and connected to their subjects.

Yet, the current Christian theory of evil is, in principle, no different from the witch theory of evil, which goes something like this: Bad things happen because of the "fall" in the Garden of Eden and the "original sin" we are born with because we have fallen away from God. Thus, we are free to sin and do evil, and Satan is real and still operates in the world. The solution to this evil is to accept the sacrifice of the deity, which exonerates you from anything you did in your life, no matter how evil it might have been. This makes Christianity a cult of human sacrifice. But instead of the sacrifice of children or beasts of burden as practiced by primitive religions, the updated 2.0 version is the sacrifice of one child—the Son of God. This leads to what I call "the identity crisis problem":

1. We were originally created sinless, but because God gave us free will and Adam and Eve chose to eat the forbidden fruit of the knowledge of good and evil, we are all born with original sin.

2. God being omnipotent and omnibenevolent could just forgive the sins we never committed, but instead he sacrificed his Son Jesus, who is actually just himself in the flesh, because Christians believe in only one god—monotheism—of which Jesus and the Holy Spirit are just different manifestations: three in one, one in three.

3. The only way to avoid eternal punishment for sins we never committed from this all-powerful and all-loving God is to accept his Son—who is actually himself—as our savior.

4. So, God sacrificed himself to himself to save us from himself.

If someone made this argument in a different context we would consider him barking mad!

And if you don't accept the logic of this proposition, you get to spend forever in hell, your flesh seared by fire for all eternity. Why? Because God loves you! Jesus himself said: "If you do not remain in me, you are like a branch that is thrown away and withers; such branches are picked up, thrown into the fire and burned" (John 15:6). In other words, "believe in me *or else!*"

In addition to explaining specific acts of evil that refuted the witch theory of causality—such as earthquakes, tsunamis, plagues, and accidents—science also gives us a more cogent understanding of evil itself, which I outlined in my 2003 book *The Science of Good and Evil*. What science tells us is that the religious supernatural theory of evil is false. It's a myth. It's what I call "the myth of pure evil." The myth of pure evil is the belief that evil exists separately from individuals, or that evil exists within people as something like what we traditionally think of as an evil "force," driving them to perform evil acts. "Evil" as a noun implies an existence all its own, as in an "evil force" or even an "evil person," or "the force in nature that governs and gives rise to wickedness and sin," or "the wicked or immoral part of someone or something," and so on in its dictionary form.

In this latter sense I claim that there is no such thing as evil. There is no supernatural force operating outside the realm of the known laws of nature and human behavior that we can call evil. Calling something or someone "evil" gets us nowhere. It leads to no greater understanding. In a scientific sense it is a term ultimately indefinable. That is, there is no way to establish quantifiable criteria by which we may distinguish between something or someone that is "evil" or "not evil," or shades of evil in between. The tendency to use the term at all comes from our Western Platonic tendency to think in terms of essences, or non-changing "things" or "types" that are what they are by their very nature. Analogously, evil is not a fixed entity or essence.

It is not a thing. Evil is a descriptive term for a range of environmental events and human behaviors that we describe and interpret as bad, wrong, awful, undesirable, or whatever appropriately descriptive adjective or synonym for evil is chosen. To call something "evil" does not lead us to a deeper understanding of the cause of evil behavior.

If there were no humans there would be no evil. Earthquakes that kill people are not, in and of themselves, evil. A shift between two tectonic plates that causes the earth to make a sudden and dramatic movement cannot possibly be considered evil outside the effects such an earthquake might have on the humans living near the fault line.

It is the effects of the earthquake on our fellow humans that we judge to be evil. Evil as a physical concept requires human evaluation of a behavior and its effects on humans. As such, bacterial diseases cannot be inherently evil. By causing humans to sneeze, cough, vomit, and have diarrhea, bacteria are highly successful organisms, spreading themselves far and wide. As their human hosts, we may label the effects of a disease as evil, but the disease itself has no moral existence. Good and evil are human constructs.

At the end of an informal debate with Dr. Huffling I told him "I'd like to steel man your argument but I honestly have no idea what your position is. Can you just explain to me please, why God does not cure childhood leukemia? These innocent children suffer horribly and the lives of their parents are in agony forever at the loss of their children. God could intervene. Why doesn't he?" Huffling's answer: "I don't know."[3]

---

3. "If God, Why Evil?," 1:02:24.

Part I: The Debate

From my perspective, if you don't know, if the only answer—no matter how loaded with philosophical jargon it is—comes down to "God works in mysterious ways" and "who can understand God," you don't have a case. The only logical conclusion is, as far as I can see (and I've read all the arguments trying to square the circle of evil), there either is no God, or there are multiple gods (some good, some evil), or the God of process theology is true and God simply cannot do anything about evil as it is not yet in his power to act.

2

God Is Not a Moral Being[1]

J. Brian Huffling

It might be pertinent if I lay out some agreements between me and Dr. Shermer. First, we both agree that evil is not a thing in itself (I will provide a definition of evil later). Evil is not an entity or a noun, but an adjective that describes something. Second, we both believe, albeit for different reasons, that morality is something known rather intuitively. Third, we both take morality to be objective. Now for the more interesting stuff: the differences.

The topic of our discussion was "Is the Reality of Evil Good Evidence Against the Christian God?" There is a lot to unpack here. For starters, it should be firmly grasped that discussions about God and evil are inherently philosophical in nature. This was one of my main points in the debate. But what do I mean by "philosophical"? Probably not what Shermer thought I meant. It seems that he equates philosophy in general with analytic philosophy in particular. The latter is basically the reduction of philosophical concepts to language (analyzing terms, their definitions, and their relationships to other words/ideas). Doubtless there are many philosophers who are analytic, especially in the U.S. However, this is not what philosophy has been traditionally and historically.

Traditionally, philosophy has been a rational investigation into such areas as the nature of being/existence (metaphysics), the nature of

---

1. This chapter is adapted from Huffling, "Reality of Evil."

knowledge (epistemology), etc., and any number of sub-disciplines such as the philosophy of math, philosophy of science, or the philosophy of religion.

Philosophy asks questions about the nature of things. For example, what is the nature of reality/existence, knowledge, and truth? Do universals—such as redness, humanness, and circularity—exist in some way? Whereas science studies things in nature, philosophy of science asks about the nature of science and scientific knowledge, such as what counts as science? One position that has been popular in this regard says that something counts as scientific if it can be falsifiable. In Shermer's chapter he brings up "Sagan's dragon."[2] I won't retell that story here except to say that the dragon can't be empirically falsified in any way and therefore is said not to exist. According to Shermer, Sagan's point is that if something can't be falsified it can't count as knowledge. Shermer cites Sagan's *The Demon-Haunted World* to illustrate the necessity of falsifiability in order to attain reliable knowledge."[3] I do not disagree with this; however, I wouldn't take "falsifiability" to be merely empirical in nature as something can be falsified rationally—i.e., it can be shown to be contradictory or internally inconsistent. But note that this principle is not an empirical assertion—it is a philosophical one. It asserts something about the nature of knowledge.

My point with all this is that philosophy is not mere logic chopping or language games (even though some philosophers have wrongly reduced it to that). A quick scanning of the history of philosophy will prove as much. Thinkers like Plato, Aristotle, Plotinus, Augustine, Anselm, Aquinas, Locke, Hume, Kant, etc., did not merely play language games but interacted with highly philosophical notions.

I have been using the word "science" but have not yet defined it. I think Shermer and I will agree on a basic definition of science that is fairly commonsensical. I take science (in the modern sense of the word) to be the empirical investigation of the natural world. Science is certainly an empirical investigation (even if not all of what it studies can be visually perceptible; consider, for instance, atoms, virtual particles, and the like). If science is indeed a study of the natural world via the senses, then by definition it is locked into studying the physical universe and nothing that is not part of the physical universe. I don't think any natural scientist would object to this caricature. But if science studies only the natural world, then natural

2. *God, Evil, and Morality*, 5–6.
3. *God, Evil, and Morality*, 5–6.

science *by definition* will not tell us about the existence of God (unless we posit God as material or part of the universe, which I am not doing). If God is immaterial, then he will not fall under the purview of natural science.

Such is not a knock against natural science. There are plenty of areas that philosophy cannot help with, such as my vision, getting your car fixed, animal behavior, etc. One field is not necessarily "better" than the other; they are just different regarding their domains. But the point is, natural science cannot inform us about the existence of God, and Shermer conceded this point in our in-person discussion.

I would also submit that the notion of "evil" is not something that natural science can tell us about, at least not regarding its philosophical nature. Of course, and as Shermer points out lucidly, science can tell us about genetic problems, physiological problems, behavioral issues, etc., and all of these either are or could result in evil. But *evil* in the sense of having a *value* is not a scientific idea. The notions of good and evil are *value* terms, not subject to empirical investigation. This is not to say that scientists can't tell us that an *x* is a good or bad member of its species, or whatever it is. But saying that something is behaviorally good, bad, or evil is not merely a scientific notion. These terms are about the nature of things. When we call something *good* we are referring to something beyond its physical properties. We can certainly limit the term "good" to physical properties when we say that someone has a good arm, for example, as a baseball pitcher does. But when we describe behavior or a state of being, we are saying something beyond such properties. When a child contracts some kind of disease, we call that an evil. But this goes beyond a mere scientific description and provides a value to the situation. Such values are intertwined with science but are not merely scientific.

So then what is "evil"? Shermer defined evil as intentional harm against sentient beings.[4] I would agree that such would be evil. But the word has a deeper, philosophical meaning. We can talk about natural evils and moral evils. The former would include natural disasters and diseases, while the latter has to do with evil and suffering caused by someone's bad behavior. Shermer and I agree that tornadoes and such things are not evil *in and of themselves*. However, the destruction they bring about and the death they cause are evils (although he may reserve the term "evil" for moral issues). To better understand what I mean by evil may require a discussion on the nature of God and how he differs from nature.

---

4. "If God, Why Evil?," 7:43.

For the sake of space I cannot go into theistic proofs for God's existence; I am merely going to explain the classical view of God as we believe him to exist *per* these proofs. (The interested reader can read Brian Davies' *Introduction to the Philosophy of* Religion 4th edition for a discussion of said proofs.) If our arguments for God are sound, then God is not part of this universe. He is the creator of all aspects of our known world, which would include matter, time, change, etc. If God is the cause of such things, he could not be material, temporal, changing, etc. We argue that God is an immaterial, spaceless, timeless, unchanging being. Such a being is being itself, lacking nothing. He is infinite in the sense that he is not limited by anything. He is perfect, metaphysically speaking, since he is complete unbounded existence. This is what we mean by *perfection* regarding God.

If something exists, it has something good. *Existence* itself is good. From a theistic point of view, to have existence is to be like God (in a very qualified way), which is a good thing. "Evil" in the philosophical sense is some corruption of a good thing. As Shermer has said, there is nothing that is pure evil. Traditional theists would agree. Even something that has been corrupted, such as an immoral human, would have aspects of goodness, such as existence. On this view evil can't be a thing in itself since it would have to exist. If existence is a good thing, then it would be contradictory to call something pure evil, as it would have to exist, which in itself is a good.

So how does God relate to evil? A traditional response is that God created mankind with free will, and man somehow willed something that he was commanded not to, which resulted in moral corruption (evil). Thus, was the introduction of sin, which also caused sickness, disease, and death. While Shermer does not like this explanation, there is nothing illogical with it. If one rejects theism, then it seems impossible, which it would be if God didn't exist. However, if theism is true, there is nothing far-fetched about this scenario. The question is: "Is theism true?" I would argue that it is, but since our discussion is not about God's existence *per se*, I need to remain on the actual topic, which is "Is evil evidence against God?"

The next question to ask is, "What would have to be the case for the problem of evil to count as evidence against God?" Since Shermer has laid out the problem of evil I will not do so here. I have no objection to how he explained the argument. The main thrust of the problem is to show that given the existence of evil, a God that is all-knowing, all-powerful, and all-good could not exist. (This is just one form of the argument. The logical problem is the form Shermer has chosen, and it is the "stronger" of the two general forms in that it attempts to show that God and evil are logically contradictory. Given the existence of evil, the existence of God is impossible. The weaker form, the inductive or evidential problem, only attempts to show that God's existence is not likely given the existence of evil.)

To make the argument work, Shermer would have to show that there is indeed a logical contradiction between the existence of evil and the God just described. However, many philosophers, even atheists, have conceded that there is no logical contradiction between evil and God's existence. That is, there is nothing that is logically required of evil given the existence of God.

Premise 1 of the first argument Shermer uses asserts that God is morally perfect.[5] Premise 4 states that such a being would desire to eliminate all evil. Taken with the other premises, God is said not to exist. The conditional argument (the third one he gives) says the same thing in premise 2: "If God is all good, *should* he not prevent evil from existing?" In our debate, Shermer said that if God did exist we should expect the universe to be different than it is.[6] Since it's not, then God is said not to exist. Such is the linchpin of the problem of evil: God *should* solve the issue of evil, and we think God *should* act differently than he is, therefore, he doesn't exist.

My point by way of response is this: if God is the creator of the universe, then he does not have properties of creation. Morality is a property of creation. Therefore, God does not have moral properties (i.e., he is not a moral being). Notice what I'm not saying. I'm not saying that God is evil; I'm saying he is not the type of being to be moral. I am also not denying that he is good. But I am denying that whatever his goodness means is a result of behaving a certain way. Let's look at each of these points in turn.

When I say that God is not a moral being what I am saying is that he does not have moral obligations to anything or anyone. As humans we have moral obligations. We *ought* to act a certain way. However, I would argue that this is because we have a particular human nature that is objective and the same across cultures and time. Humans require certain goods to flourish and be happy, as Shermer rightly points out. Causing harm and obstructing such goods from being attained is an evil. Further, we know what humans are *supposed to be like*. But what sense does that talk make when applied to the creator?

First, God does not need anything in order to flourish. If he is perfect being as such, he doesn't need anything. There is also no standard which

---

5. *God, Evil, and Morality*, 3.
6. "If God, Why Evil?," 9:37.

he is obligated to maintain. When one says, "God ought to do x," what does *ought* mean here? I would say that it means, we think we know how God should act because we know how humans should act, and he isn't acting in a way that would be appropriate for a human. *But God is not a human.* While we know the nature of humans and know what a human should be like in terms of behavior, *we don't know what God is like in this way*. We have no direct knowledge of God. Our knowledge of God is from his effects, namely, the universe. So, while empirical science studies his effects directly, philosophy studies God *from his effects*. In other words, we argue that if the effects are caused by something that is not identical with them, then the cause can't have those same properties. For example, if the effects are physical, then God can't be physical. If all material things as such were created, then God couldn't be material since then *all material things as such* would not have been created. He would have been one of those things. However, such is impossible since we know that there can't be an infinite regress of one material thing causing another material thing. The same can be said for changing beings, temporal beings, or contingent beings.

The point of all this is that we don't have direct knowledge of God the way we have direct knowledge of the universe. This seems to be a mark against God's existence, according to Shermer when he asks, "What's the difference between this an invisible non-acting God and there's just no God at all?"[7] Or what is the difference between such a God and Sagan's dragon?[8] Well, as I said in our discussion, there is no positive evidence for such a dragon; however, there is evidence for a God. Such evidence is a *demonstratio quia* type of reasoning, which means we argue from the effect to the cause. This is actually done in science when one can see the effect but not the cause. The cause is reasoned to from the effect, such as we see in arguments for virtual particles or black holes. Those can't be seen, but their existence explains the data. So this is not an unfamiliar way of arguing for scientists.

At this point in the oral debate, Shermer argues that the petitionary prayer examples show God hasn't done anything measurable to prove his existence.[9] However, I would submit that *even if God did reach out in an answered prayer* in some miraculous sense, *we still couldn't measure God as the cause of such a miracle.* The effect could be measured, but God *as the cause of the effect* could never be measured, even in principle. Thus, God is not a thing

---

7. "If God, Why Evil?," 16:39. and *God, Evil, and Morality*, 6.
8. *God, Evil, and Morality*, 6.
9. "If God, Why Evil?," 51:31.

to be measured via empirical means. We can only say what God is by looking at his effects and reasoning back to the nature of the cause. (However, Christians would say that God did step into nature as Jesus, and in other ways.)

Let's examine some of the words we use to describe God: immaterial, infinite, eternal, impassible, and immutable. These are not positive words or descriptions of what God is but are negative words about what he is not. In order, these words mean "not material," "not finite," "not temporal," "not affected," and "not changeable." We can use positive words for God, such as being, goodness, perfect, etc. However, even with these words we have to understand that they don't mean the exact same thing when applied to limited, finite beings (things in the universe) and an unlimited, infinite being (God).

Let's examine the word "good." I can say the following things are good: shoes, a car, a person, a cheeseburger, a golf shot. The same word (good) is applied to all of these, but it should be clear that the meaning is not exactly the same in all cases. What makes these things good are not the same. In other words, shoes are good because of their comfort and protection. A car is good if it functions like it should. A person is good if he or she acts in the way he or she should. A cheeseburger is good if it is nutritious and tasty. A golf shot is good if it accomplishes what it set out to. So, the word "good" is not used in the same way when applied to all of these words. It is used kind of the same way, but not exactly. In other words, it is used analogously. What every example has in common with the word "good" is that we know what each of these things *should be*. If it is that way, then it is said to be good. We have some knowledge of their natures. We know these things directly.

We *do not* have such knowledge of God. Our knowledge of him is not direct, and we certainly don't know what he is in his nature. As finite beings we cannot *even in principle* know the infinity of God. This is not a mark against his existence; it is an admission of a qualified agnosticism regarding *what he is*, not *that he is*. If we as finite beings knew what God was exactly, he would not be much of a God.

This is not to say God is not good; it just means that "good" is not meant in a moral sense. Classical theists maintain that God is metaphysically good in that he is complete being without any corruption or lack. Remember, that was the definition of evil. If God is completely devoid of evil, he is completely good, albeit because of the *kind of being* he is, not because he behaves in a certain way. Rather than saying that such a lack of morality is a deficiency, as some will protest, it is actually a perfection. Humans can be good or evil, but God cannot even possibly be evil. His goodness is one with his act of pure being and is not dependent, as it is with us on behavior.

The point: we don't know what God *should* be like, or that he even should be like anything. So we can't say that God *should* behave in a certain way or do certain things. But this is exactly what the problem of evil is all about: saying what God should do and how he should behave.

If what I have been saying is true, we just took away a major premise of the problem of evil. As atheist J. L. Mackie asserted, doing this keeps the problem from even arising. Thus, there is no contradiction between God's existence and evil. Remember, this discussion was initially about whether evil serves as evidence against God's existence, not about answering questions about why God does or doesn't do something.

Science can't study God, and as I have pointed out, the argument Shermer presents does not eliminate a metaphysically good God. The problem of evil centers around how we think God *ought* to act. But if what I have been saying is right, we can't say God *ought* to do anything. This doesn't answer the question as to why God allows evil, but that was not the point of the discussion. It does show that God's existence is not negated by evil. As I said in the debate, evil does not invalidate other arguments for God's existence. If such arguments are sound, then we have positive reasons for believing that God exists. Not knowing *why* God allows evil is not evidence that he isn't there.

Shermer has made much of my admission (taken somewhat out of the overall context) that we don't know why God doesn't heal people, child leukemia as an example. The only way we could know this answer is to know the mind of God. However, such an admission does not in any way negate God's existence, especially in light of what I have said about God. However, let me offer a couple of reasons as to why he might not heal. First, as I said in the debate, if God answered every prayer offered, a multitude every second around the world, then he would alter the natural course of the world. The natural world being altered at such a rate would result in two problems: one, it would be the end of the natural order if God supernaturally intervenes every second. There would be no natural order to speak of. Two, it would eradicate the very significance of miracles as supernatural acts by God for some end.

Contrary to popular belief, people in the biblical world did not expect a miracle every day. Miracles were very few and far between in the 1,500 or so year span from the beginning to the end of the Bible. Most miracles centered around Moses/Aaron, Elijah/Elisha, and Jesus/the apostles. A miracle was simply not a normal event, even for people living in the biblical times. This is why people were so astounded at the miracles of Jesus: they hadn't seen anything like it before. God did not do miracles just for the sake of miracles. The Greek word for "miracle" also means "sign." That's how miracles function: as signs for something, like the deity of Christ. They authenticated what he did and what he said about himself. However, if miracles happened all the time, they would lose such force. They would just be seen as normal events and lose all of their authenticating purpose. I would even doubt if people who identify as skeptics would take these events as supernatural since their cause could not be measured and they would just be seen as part of nature given their regularity.

Having said this, the Christian message is that God will in fact bring healing. The fact that he has not yet done so does not mean he won't somehow. While I certainly agree with Shermer that people need help from medicine and science, that does not mean they don't need spiritual help too. Such is a false dichotomy. Christians believe that disease and death are consequences of our rebellion against God (a.k.a. sin). But disease and death are not the end of the Christian story.

The bottom line for the alleged lack of verification from petitionary prayer and healing is this: they don't prove God doesn't exist. Other independent arguments are made for God, and evil does not invalidate them. Finally, God is not subject to our desires or what we think he ought to do. The creator of the universe does not answer to us. The Book of Job makes this point very well.

Regarding the irrefutable God problem, as Shermer calls it, no serious philosopher of religion makes an argument for God based on such reasoning. I would also point out that God does in fact get a lot of blame for bad things happening, so I think his assertion here is demonstrably false.

The identity crisis problem regarding the Trinity demonstrates a lack of understanding regarding the orthodox Christian view of God. In fact, Shermer's illustration of the Trinity is more akin to the ancient heresy of modalism, which is rejected by Christians, than to the historical view.

Such only scratches the surface. For the interested reader I would commend Brian Davies' book, *The Reality of God and the Problem of Evil*.

3

Harm and the Definition of God[1]

GARY J. WHITTENBERGER

IN THE LAST CHAPTER, theologian Brian Huffling presented his answer to the question "Is the reality of evil good evidence against the Christian God?" Although Huffling does yeoman's work in his attempt to justify the negative answer, in the end his defense fails. The evidence cited by Shermer is not only good, it is decisive. It shows that God does not exist!

What is evil anyway? Shermer defined it as "intentional harm against sentient beings."[2] I think this is a pretty good modern definition, but Huffling doesn't buy it. He wants to hang on to an older concept that asserts that even natural disasters, like destructive hurricanes, are evil. Of course, if a god were to cause destructive hurricanes, then they would be evil by Shermer's definition, since the god would have intended these harms. "Evil" is primarily a religious concept and has different meanings even among theists. Huffling himself equivocates on the term in his own essay.

I think it is time to discard the idea of evil in discussions of the existence of God. Let's simplify and ask: "Does the fact that humans are significantly harmed in many specific ways count as evidence against God?" Or, to put it more bluntly, "Do significant specific harms to humans prove that God does not exist?" Furthermore, let's forthrightly rename the associated argument to "The argument from harm against the existence of God."

---

1. This chapter is adapted from Whittenberger, "Does God Exist?"
2. "If God, Why Evil?," 7:43.

We must begin with a definition of "God." Here I am going to use one derived from holy books, from writings of philosophers, theologians, and religious leaders over the centuries, and from modern surveys of lay persons. "God" is the hypothetical eternal, all-knowing, all-powerful, perfectly moral being or agent who created our universe and sometimes intervenes in it. This is the god believed in by most Jews, Christians, and Muslims. Although this definition will not satisfy all, I believe it will satisfy most theists, atheists, and agnostics. Starting with this standard definition I believe I can demonstrate that God does not exist.

Some of the older versions of the argument from harm referred to *all* evil, suffering, harm, or pain, but I don't think this is necessary. Modern versions that refer to specific classes of harm, or even specific instances of harm, are more clear, concise, and powerful. Along these lines I will present three versions here:

Tsunami version:

1. If God did exist, then the Great Southeast Asia Tsunami of December 2004 would not have occurred.
2. The Great Southeast Asia Tsunami of December 2004 did occur.[3]
3. Therefore, God does not exist.

Holocaust version:

1. If God did exist, then the Holocaust would not have occurred.
2. The Holocaust did occur.
3. Therefore, God does not exist.

Rape version:

1. If God did exist, then men would never rape women.
2. Some men rape women.
3. Therefore, God does not exist.

These are all variations of a *modus tollens* type of argument. The logic is valid. If both premises (#1 and #2) are true, then the conclusion (#3) is true. The second premise in all three arguments is undoubtedly true, although there is still a small number of Holocaust deniers in the world.

---

3. Augustyn, "Indian Ocean Tsunami of 2004," *Encyclopaedia Britannica*.

Christians like Huffling, and other theists, would certainly claim that the first premises are false, but they are mistaken. Here's why.

Supporting these first premises is a line of reasoning that goes like this: If God did exist, during his act (or acts) of creation of the universe, he would not create or allow for events like the 2004 tsunami, the Holocaust, or men who rape women. Why? Because God would be perfectly moral, and perfectly moral beings do not and would not intentionally create conditions that cause harm to other beings, if they can avoid it. And God could avoid it because he would be all-powerful.

Floundering in religious babble, Huffling attempts to defeat this reasoning by switching out his god for a different god, one less able and less worthy of our worship. He says, "I'm not saying that God is evil; I'm saying he is not the type of being to be moral. I am also not denying that he is good. But I am denying that whatever his goodness means is a result of behaving a certain way."[4] This is unpersuasive. Since God would be a being or intelligent agent, he would be the type of being or agent who would behave morally or immorally. In fact, since he would be perfectly moral, he would behave morally in all situations.

For God, Huffling tries to substitute a deity who is exempt from and somehow beyond objective morality. Digging himself a deeper hole, Huffling then says, "When I say that God is not a moral being what I am saying is that he does not have moral obligations to anything or anyone. As humans we have moral obligations. We ought to act a certain way. . . . Further, we know what humans are *supposed to be like*. But what sense does that talk make when applied to the creator?"[5] It makes a lot of sense! We know what God is supposed to be like because we can refer to the standard definition of "God."

According to objective morality, to which both Huffling and Shermer assent, all beings or intelligent agents have moral obligations to all other beings or intelligent agents, and one of these moral obligations is to not cause harm to others if you can avoid it. Unfortunately, Huffling is a proponent of a view I call "divine exceptionalism." This is the idea that gods (currently hypothetical beings), because of their immense power, authority, or creativity, are or should be exempted from objective morality. But just like presidents should not be above the law, gods or other nonhuman beings should not be above morality. Divine exceptionalism is totally unacceptable

---

4. *God, Evil, and Morality*, 15.
5. *God, Evil, and Morality*, 15. Emphasis in original.

to reasonable people. If Huffling wants to defend an amoral god, let him do so, but then he is no longer talking about God, or at least the Christian god he defends. The argument from harm clearly shows that God does not exist. Huffling continues:

> [W]e think we know how God should act because we know how humans should act, and he isn't acting in a way that would be appropriate for a human. *But God is not a human.* While we know the nature of humans and know what a human should be like in terms of behavior, *we don't know what God is like in this way.*[6]

Yes, if God did exist, he would not be a human. Nevertheless, God would fall into the class of "beings or intelligent agents," and we know how they should behave and not behave. We don't *know* what God is like in any way; we don't *know* that God even exists. However, we *know* what God *would* be like with respect to his behavior towards other beings or intelligent agents because we have a definition of "God" that includes "perfectly moral" as a descriptor. Other descriptors that could be used here and have been used by theists include "perfectly good," "all-loving," and "omnibenevolent," but they all imply the same behavior towards others.

Huffling treads on thin ice when he talks about science. He says, "If science is indeed a study of the natural world by means of the senses, then by definition it is locked into studying the physical universe but not anything that is not part of the physical universe."[7] That is a narrow caricature of science. It would be better to say that science is the study of *reality* by means of the senses and rational inference. If God is a real thing, and his interactions and effects are broad enough, then he should be amenable to detection and inference by us. There is no reason why his alleged existence cannot be studied by science. The late Victor Stenger, a well-respected physicist, made this case in a few of his books.[8]

Michael Shermer brings out very good scientific evidence against the existence of God by pointing to the empirical studies of so-called "intercessory prayer." These studies show that prayer doesn't work. And so, science and philosophy can be combined to formulate a different but similar kind of argument against the existence of God, as follows:

---

6. *God, Evil, and Morality*, 16. Emphasis in original.
7. *God, Evil, and Morality*, 12.
8. Stenger, *God, the Failed Hypothesis.*

1. If God did exist, then he would favorably respond to intercessory prayers for healing.
2. If he would respond favorably to such prayers, then the rate of good outcomes for heart patients would be much higher for an experimental group (prayed for) than for a control group (not prayed for) in a well-designed scientific experiment.
3. However, in an experiment like this, i.e., the Benson study,[9] the rate of good outcomes for the experimental group was slightly *lower* than the rate for the control group.
4. Therefore, God does not exist.

Huffling's response to the prayer studies is weak:

> However, let me offer a couple of reasons as to why he [God] might not heal. First, as I said in the debate, if God answered every prayer offered, a multitude every second around the world, then he would alter the natural course of the world. The natural world being altered at such a rate would result in two problems: one, it would be the end of the natural order if God supernaturally intervenes every second. There would be no natural order to speak of. Two, it would eradicate the very significance of miracles as supernatural acts by God for some end.[10]

Once again, Huffling tries to switch gods on us. He tries to delete the omnipotence trait from the definition of "God" and adopt a lesser god. However, if God did exist, he could preserve an order to the universe while healing human persons of a particular ailment and could still perform miracles, just a different kind of miracle. When challenged by the argument from harm, theists like Huffling just try to move back the goal posts as atheists prepare to kick the winning field goal. Theists simply break the rules of reason.

Huffling's objections crumble once again when he says, "[T]he Christian message is that God will in fact bring healing. The fact that he has not yet done so does not mean he won't somehow."[11] If God did exist, we wouldn't be asking questions like "Why hasn't God healed cancer in children?" or "Will God *somehow* heal cancer in children?" God would not

---

9. Benson et al., "Intercessory Prayer," 934–42.
10. *God, Evil, and Morality*, 18.
11. *God, Evil, and Morality*, 19.

have created a world in which there is cancer in children! Why? Because he would be both all-powerful and perfectly moral. Beings who are morally infallible creators do not create conditions that produce cancer in children.

The Holocaust and rape arguments that I presented earlier, unlike the tsunami argument, involve the aggression of humans against other humans. Like Plantinga[12] and other theists, Huffling follows the free-will blame-the-victim trope:

> So how does God relate to evil? A traditional response is that God created mankind with free will, and man somehow willed something that he was commanded not to, which resulted in moral corruption (evil). Thus, was the introduction of sin, which also caused sickness, disease, and death.[13]

So humans, not God, are to blame? The concept of free will is controversial in itself, but for the sake of argument, here let's assume that humans have a kind of libertarian free will, as most Christians claim. That is, they make free choices and are therefore volitional beings. If God did exist, he would not have given to humans the free will to exterminate Jews, nor would he have given to men the free will to rape women, because God would have been all-powerful and perfectly moral. He would have prevented these particular horrible kinds of harm *by design*. If God did exist, he would have created the brains of humans such that physical aggression would not even come to mind. Also, the Christian idea that God would punish descendants of Adam and Eve for the sins of this couple, if they existed, is ridiculous in itself. Such action would violate the principle of individual accountability in objective morality. God would not do this since he would be perfectly moral.

There are many other problems in Huffling's response to Shermer, e.g., vagueness, equivocation, irrelevance, ignoring evidence, etc., but it would take too much space and time to identify, describe, and correct all these problems. The main point here is that Huffling's objections to the various versions of the argument from harm fail miserably. If God did exist, things would be different from the way they are. Therefore, God does not exist. If Huffling and others want to abandon their god and try to defend the existence of a lesser god, fine, but this does not alter the conclusion that

---

12. Plantinga, *God, Freedom, and Evil.*
13. *God, Evil, and Morality*, 14.

God does not exist. Philosophy and science together lead us to the correct conclusion.

4

Rejecting Divine Exceptionalism[1]

J. Brian Huffling

My first chapter was a response to Michael Shermer who had argued in his piece that examples of evil in the world demonstrate God does not exist. His basic point was if God exists, he would not allow evil. In short, my response was we don't have knowledge of what God is. We can't assume that God is like humans. We cannot say *a priori* that God is a moral being. Thus, it would be wrong to say (without argument) that God is beholden to human standards of behavior. Thus, it would be presumptuous to say what God would or would not do.

Whittenberger affirms if God exists, then he would be a moral being. Before I respond to that I think it is pertinent to address two definitional issues. First, in defining "evil," Whittenberger appears to think I reject Shermer's definition for my "older concept." If he is rejecting my position simply because it is older, that is an example of the fallacy of chronological snobbery. I do not reject Shermer's definition, though. I simply think it is too narrow. I certainly agree that intentional harm (by humans) against sentient beings is evil. I also do not think that natural disasters in themselves constitute moral evil. However, they could *cause* evil by harming sentient creatures. (Although this would be in the category of what philosophers often call physical evil, not moral evil.) While Whittenberger seemingly denies natural disasters are evil, his first argument against God's existence

---

1. This chapter is adapted from Huffling, "God Is Not a Moral Being."

is from a natural disaster. Apparently, his response would be it is evil only if it is intentional and that if God did exist, then he wouldn't create the very conditions for such events. However, such begs the question. Whittenberger's definition of God already posits that God would have to behave like a human. However, the whole thrust of my last chapter was to argue that God is not required to act like we do; after all, he is not a human. My point is that Whittenberger seems to have an underlying view that natural disasters are evil (even if not in the moral sense) in that they bring about death and suffering. But such harkens back to the "older concept" of evil.

In a curious statement Whittenberger claims, "'Evil' is primarily a religious concept and has different meanings even among theists."[2] He writes, "I think it is time to discard the idea of evil in discussions of the existence of God."[3] He wants to shift the argument from *evil* to *harm*. This seems like a distinction without a difference since harm would apparently be evil if God intentionally allows it. Further, the issue of evil is a philosophical concept and has been discussed by philosophers who are not religious (e.g., Hume and Mackie).

At this point Whittenberger defines God as an "eternal, all-knowing, all-powerful, perfectly moral being."[4] He rightly notes that this is the typical view of God as described by philosophers, etc. To be sure, most Christians define God in such a way—although these concepts have become debatable even among theists. The main thrust of my original article (and debate with Shermer) was that God is not a moral being with obligations to others. My argument was that since God is not a human, he does not have a human nature or a moral nature (like humans). Thus, the problem of evil that is based on God being immoral for allowing evil (or harm) fails. Further, there are a number of philosophers and theologians who agree that God is indeed not a moral being; rather, he transcends morality in the way he transcends space, time, and matter.[5]

Whittenberger declares, "Starting with this standard definition I believe I can demonstrate that God does not exist."[6] If I have only one point to make as a way of critique regarding Whittenberger's article, it is this: Whittenberger's way of thinking here is entirely circular. My stating that

2. *God, Evil, and Morality*, 20.
3. *God, Evil, and Morality*, 20.
4. *God, Evil, and Morality*, 21.
5. For example, see Davies, *The Reality of God*, and McCabe, *God and Evil*.
6. *God, Evil, and Morality*, 21.

God is not a moral being is the conclusion of philosophical analysis and argumentation. For Whittenberger, God being moral is simply definitional. However, this is the *entire point* of my arguments. If Whittenberger wants to critique my position, that is fine, but it simply will not do to make the central point of contention a matter of definition. The moral status of God is central to both of our positions. Neither of us can simply define God as being moral or not. Any conclusion on this matter requires philosophical analysis and demonstration.

Whittenberger's response would likely be that it is legitimate to define God in this way since so many do. However, such a manner is not how truth is discovered. There are many beliefs in history and science that the majority of people held to erroneously. If Whittenberger is going to critique my position, he is going to have to *demonstrate* that God is a moral being. Unfortunately, he does not do this; rather, he merely posits God's moral standing as a point of definition (and assumes that since God is in the class of intellectual beings then he must be moral).

He gives three arguments from harm as a way of showing God doesn't exist.[7] The basic thrust of all three goes like this:

1. If God did exist, then x would not have occurred.
2. X did occur.
3. Therefore, God does not exist.

This type of argumentation makes at least two assumptions: (1) That God is a moral being and has certain obligations to his creatures, and (2) that Whittenberger knows exactly what God is like and how he would/should behave. With all due respect to Dr. Whittenberger, it is extremely presumptuous for a limited, finite creature to know what the unlimited, infinite creator would and would not do (given his existence). There is absolutely no way we can say "If God exists, then he would have to do x, y, and z." Again, this begs the question. Further, it is a gross anthropomorphic view of God that holds God is just like us but to an infinite degree. Surely Whittenberger and I do not agree on the existence of God; however, supposing that a creator does exist, there is absolutely no reason to think he is a mirror image of us. This is very typical, however, even in evangelical thinking. But it is backwards. If we are going to try to discover what something is like, we don't form an *a priori* notion of it and then make theories about

---

7. *God, Evil, and Morality*, 21.

it. Rather, we let the data tell us what it is like. Whittenberger is forming *a priori* assumptions about what God would have to be like, rather than doing the only thing we can do regarding a study of God (apart from revealed text): study the world around us and then make philosophical (*a posteriori*) conclusions about what God is like. Ironically, I am arguing for more of a scientific view here (in the historical sense of "scientific," i.e., showing the conclusion via demonstration), while Whittenberger is being philosophically dogmatic. We should let the data inform our theories, not define our theories *a priori*.

For example, if the universe is physical, temporal, and changing, then it would need a cause. But the cause could not have those same characteristics, or we would be led into an infinite regress of causes, which is impossible. Rather, we arrive at a cause that is itself not those things. Anything with the above characteristics cannot account for itself, thus the cause of those effects cannot have such characteristics, since it too would need a cause. And isn't this what we should expect from a being we don't directly experience and is not part of nature? By the nature of reality, a finite being cannot comprehend an infinite being. If we knew exactly what God was like, he wouldn't be much of a God (*contra* Whittenberger).

Whittenberger's underlying reason for God not allowing evil is that he believes God would be perfectly moral and not able to allow it. At this point Whittenberger makes what I think is probably his most egregious statement: that I am trying "to defeat [his] reasoning by switching out [my] god for a different god, one less able and less worthy of our worship."[8] This is quite puzzling because philosophers and theologians have historically argued the opposite: that the more God is like us the more he is like a created, finite being. However, the more he is not limited like us, the greater he is. The god Whittenberger is describing is more limited than the one I am arguing for. Rather than saying God must do x, y, or z, I am arguing that God is not limited by what limits us. Thus, God is actually more able and worthy of worship.

Whittenberger states that my position "is unpersuasive."[9] That is not an argument or a logical critique. For what it's worth, I find his position unpersuasive as well. But since this is a philosophical issue, my hope is to use philosophical demonstration, not merely rhetoric.

---

8. *God, Evil, and Morality*, 22.
9. *God, Evil, and Morality*, 22.

Whittenberger states that since God is intelligent, he necessarily is moral.[10] There is, however, no logical or metaphysical necessity for such an assertion. I have argued in my previous chapter that humans are moral given their nature. Our morality is based on our behavior. Our goodness is dependent, finite, and achieved. The type of God I am arguing for is a being of infinite existence, and his goodness is not dependent on what he does. He does not achieve goodness like humans do; he is goodness through his very nature of pure being (this is metaphysical, not moral goodness).

In a blatant case of begging the question, Whittenberger states, "We know what God is supposed to be like because we can refer to the standard definition of 'God.'"[11] In other words, "We know God is moral because we can define him that way." A clearer picture of circularity could not be had. Whittenberger would be right to call me out if I took a side on a debated issue in psychology simply because I wanted to define the issue a certain way. Yet, that is exactly what he is doing here.

At this point he accuses me of divine exceptionalism.[12] He claims that "all beings or intelligent agents have moral obligations to all other beings."[13] What I am accused of is saying God *should be* excepted from this rule. However, I am not saying God *should be* excepted. I'm saying he *can't* be included. It is simply a *non sequitur* to say that created beings are x, therefore creators are x. In fact, even the meaning of "intelligent" would only be analogous between a creature and God. We can say that humans think, but if God is outside of time and is changeless, then he can't think discursively. Thus, even the meaning of "knowledge" is different given a clear creator/creature distinction. However, since Whittenberger sees no distinction, God is just a big human. Certainly, God and man are not intelligent in the same way. I am arguing the difference is not merely in degree, but in kind (after all, they are radically different *kinds* of beings). Whittenberger has ignored the entire tradition of apophatic theology that spans millennia. This tradition argues that we have to negate certain characteristics that God could not have (such as being temporal, changing, or moral).

"Divine Exceptionalism," he says, "is totally unacceptable to reasonable people."[14] This is an example of the logical fallacy of poisoning the well. In

10. *God, Evil, and Morality*, 22.
11. *God, Evil, and Morality*, 22.
12. *God, Evil, and Morality*, 22.
13. *God, Evil, and Morality*, 22.
14. *God, Evil, and Morality*, 22–23.

other words, if one wants to be a reasonable person, then one can't say God is different from other intelligent beings. If one does, then by definition one is not reasonable. *Contra* Whittenberger, classical theists do not argue God is "exempted from objective morality" due to his "immense power, authority, or creativity"; rather, he is simply not a finite being and is not held to the standards that he imposes on us as finite beings. Ironically, if God were moral it would only be because he achieved it—like us. However, a more perfect goodness is to just *be* goodness in itself (again, metaphysically, not morally). The latter is a more perfect way of being (since the former would be *becoming*, not *being*).

Whittenberger states that if God did exist, he "would fall into the 'class of beings or intelligent agents,' and *we know how they should behave and not behave.*"[15] The very next statement reads: "We don't *know* what God is like in any way; we don't *know* that God even exists."[16] This admission that he doesn't know what God is like contradicts his entire chapter. To be charitable, perhaps he means we don't know what God is like since he is not an existing thing, and only existing things can be known. But this doesn't really seem to help him much since he doesn't think God exists but writes as if he does know what God is (or would be) like, and as such, *existence* doesn't seem to change what Whittenberger expects from such a being. He continues, "However, we *know* what God *would* be like with respect to his behavior towards other beings . . . because we have a definition of 'God' that includes 'perfectly moral' as a descriptor."[17] It's unclear what Whittenberger really thinks here as he is asserting flat contradictions. Either we know what God is like (or would be like) or we don't. Further, he relies on a mere definition of God to "prove" that God would be moral. Such is, again, circular reasoning.

At this point Whittenberger challenges my "caricature of science."[18] He says my definition is too narrow. His definition is "that science is the study of *reality* by means of the senses and rational inference."[19] Such a definition is surely too broad since it is indistinguishable from other subjects, such as philosophy. He asserts that if God exists, then he should be detectable and

---

15. *God, Evil, and Morality*, 23. Emphasis added.
16. *God, Evil, and Morality*, 23. Emphasis in original.
17. *God, Evil, and Morality*, 23. Emphasis in original.
18. *God, Evil, and Morality*, 23.
19. *God, Evil, and Morality*, 23. Emphasis in original.

"studied by science."[20] My point is that (natural) science studies nature. We can certainly infer God (via philosophy); however, that moves away from nature to the supernatural. Thus, by definition, natural science does not (and cannot) study the supernatural since natural science studies only nature and that via the senses.

Whittenberger's discussion of intercessory prayer results in a *non sequitur* and begs the question as to what God would do—something we shouldn't be able to know according to Whittenberger if we don't know what he is like. He claims my response to the prayer examples is weak.[21] I will just say that even granting such a position on prayer does not logically necessitate God's non-existence. Again, this begs the question. I didn't say God couldn't do anything. I merely point out in my quote that miracles would be much more ordinary if they happened all the time. If they did, then they would just be seen as normal aspects of nature and still not count as evidence for a supernatural being. This is somewhat granted by Whittenberger when he says such miracles could heal people, "just a different kind of miracle." What kind of miracle that would be is unstated and unclear. He then asserts that "[t]heists simply break the rules of reason."[22] To break a rule of reason is to violate a law of logic. That is simply not done here, and Whittenberger fails to point out which alleged rule was violated. Such assertions are merely rhetorical in hopes of gaining sympathy from readers but lack any real logical basis.

The remainder of Whittenberger's chapter rests on the same circularity that merely relies on how we *define* God that is laced throughout the entire piece.

In the end, God's existence is a question of philosophy, not natural science. Unfortunately, there is no philosophical reasoning provided by Whittenberger for God being moral; merely an *a priori* definition of God that says God is moral from which the conclusion is drawn that God is moral and would not allow evil. Since my entire argument in my original chapter was that God is not a moral being, it is disappointing that Whittenberger ignores all of my reasoning and merely asserts his position that God is moral—the very thing in question—without *any* real argumentation other than asserting that all intelligent beings are moral.

---

20. *God, Evil, and Morality*, 23.
21. *God, Evil, and Morality*, 24.
22. *God, Evil, and Morality*, 24.

5

God Is Not Huffgod

Gary J. Whittenberger

In this chapter I have decided to avoid the risks of paraphrasing Brian Huffling's statements from the last chapter and to just quote him directly. Instead of wasting words such as "Huffling says," "Huffling claims," or "Huffling declares," etc., most of the time I will just present his quotes after his last name. Since he and I have placed on ourselves a limit of four thousand words per chapter, I do not have the space to deal with all his claims and arguments and so I have selected those which seem most controversial and/or most important to the central focus of our debate.

Huffling [in describing his response to Michael Shermer]: "In short, my response was that we don't have knowledge of what God is. We can't assume that God is like humans. We cannot say *a priori* that God is a moral being. Thus, it would be wrong to say (without argument) that God is beholden to human standards of behavior. Thus, it would be presumptuous to say what God would or would not do."[1]

Of course we don't have knowledge of what God is, i.e., what his nature is, since we don't even know that God exists! We are not in an epistemological position to observe and describe the nature of God. God is not like a red-headed woodpecker, a giraffe, or a human person whose natures we can surmise after observing them. We can only speculate about what the nature of God would be like, if he were to exist. Over the millennia

---

1. *God, Evil, and Morality*, 27.

there has arisen a consensus about what God's nature would be and this has led to the standard definition of God. God is defined as a hypothetical intelligent agent with a set of characteristics, among which is God's being "perfectly moral." I have presented the short version of the standard definition in a previous chapter. Thus, contrary to Huffling's claim, we *can* say "*a priori*" in a discussion of God that he would be a moral being, if he did exist. This is just part of the standard definition. If God did exist, he would not be beholden to merely human standards of behavior, but to *universal* standards of behavior for intelligent agents. From these perfectly fine assumptions about his nature, we can predict what God would and would not do, if he did exist, since he would comply with universal moral standards 100 percent of the time.

Huffling: "I also do not think that natural disasters in themselves constitute moral evil. However, they could *cause* evil by harming sentient creatures."[2]

Huffling's understanding of evil is still confused. Natural disasters are not moral evil and they do not cause evil. Natural forces sometimes cause significant harm to human beings and other animals, and when they do, we call them "natural disasters." If some intelligent agent did cause natural disasters in the way we know them to occur, then that agent would be morally wrong. The use of the word "evil" is problematic, and we are better off using other terms like "harm" or "morally wrong" in the proper context.

Huffling: "The main thrust of my original article (and debate with Shermer) was that God is not a moral being with obligations to others. My argument was that since God is not a human, he does not have a human nature or a moral nature (like humans). Thus, the problem of evil that is based on God being immoral for allowing evil (or harm) fails. Further, there are a number of philosophers and theologians who agree that God is indeed not a moral being; rather, he transcends morality in the way he transcends space, time, and matter."[3]

We need to parse this set of confused claims. Huffling claims that "God is not a moral being" and that God "does not have a moral nature (like humans)," but what does he mean by this? What is a moral being? It is an intelligent agent who thinks about decisions within a moral framework and attempts to comply with some standard of proper conduct. A being who does not think in this way and/or who is not motivated in this way

2. *God, Evil, and Morality*, 27. Emphasis in original.
3. *God, Evil, and Morality*, 28.

may be said to be "amoral." An amoral being might not know that there are standards of conduct or may know of them but not care about them. When speaking of God, the former could not be the case since God would be all-knowing. And so, an all-knowing, amoral god would probably be apathetic or indifferent to the benefits and harms to human beings which would be caused by his acts of creation, intervention, or omission. But this is contradictory to the nature of God as he has been traditionally conceived. Indeed, God has been defined as being perfectly moral, good, benevolent, or loving. He would care to increase benefits and reduce harms for his creatures, *especially* human persons. And so, if Huffling thinks God would be amoral, he is mistaken, and he must be talking about some other god.

I shall call this god to which Huffling alludes and which he seems to believe in and worship "Huffgod," in order to contrast it with God. Unless and until Huffling provides a precise alternative definition, I shall assume that Huffgod is the hypothetical unique, eternal, all-knowing, all-powerful, *amoral* person or intelligent agent who created the universe and sometimes intervenes in our world.

Huffling: "Neither of us can simply define God as being moral or not."[4]

He is simply mistaken about this. God is a hypothetical being and various definitions of him have been proposed throughout the millennia. However, one definition has stuck. It is the definition that includes "perfectly moral," and it is the one I am using. If Huffling wants to define his own god, that is fine, but if he includes "amoral" or "not a moral being" in his definition, then he is not addressing my argument against the existence of God. He is just trying to defend the existence of Huffgod, and that misses the point.

Huffling: "If Whittenberger is going to critique my position, he is going to have to demonstrate that God is a moral being."[5]

One of my critiques of Huffling's position is that he refers to his own lesser god, i.e., Huffgod, not "God" defined in the standard manner. I am not obligated to demonstrate that God is a perfectly moral being. Most religious people assume this is the case, and I am simply running with their assumption. My obligation is just to rationally *demonstrate* that God does not exist, and that is exactly what I have done.

Huffling:

---

4. *God, Evil, and Morality*, 29.
5. *God, Evil, and Morality*, 29. Emphasis in original.

> He [Whittenberger] gives three arguments from harm as a way of showing God doesn't exist. The basic thrust of all three goes like this:
> 1. If God did exist, then x would not have occurred.
> 2. X did occur.
> 3. Therefore, God does not exist.
>
> This type of argumentation makes at least two assumptions:
> 1. That God is a moral being and has certain obligations to his creatures.
> 2. That Whittenberger knows exactly what God is like and how he would/should behave.[6]

Huffling says that my type of arguments against the existence of God make at least two assumptions, i.e., that God is a moral being and has certain obligations to his creatures and that I know exactly what God is like and how he would or should behave. With qualification I plead guilty to the first charge and not guilty to the second. Neither I nor anyone else can say what God is; we can only say what we believe God would be like if he existed. God is a hypothetical being. And according to the standard definition, God would be perfectly moral and would thus have moral obligations to his creatures. Neither I nor anybody else "knows exactly what God is like." As I've said a few times already, we cannot know what something is like when we don't even know that it exists! To imply that anybody knows what God is like is to make a straw-man argument. Huffling doesn't know. I don't know. And nobody knows.

Huffling: "... it is extremely presumptuous for a limited, finite creature to know what an unlimited, infinite creator would and would not do (given his existence). There is absolutely no way we can say 'If God exists, then he would have to do x, y, and z.' Again, this begs the question."[7]

But there certainly is a way this can be done, and I have shown the way. First you take the standard definition of God, you predict what we would expect and not expect to find in our world if God did exist, we then examine our world, and finally we find that our world does not confirm the predictions. Once again, however, Huffling attempts to use a vague unstandardized definition of God as "an unlimited, infinite creator," and so it is easy to see how he goes astray. He is making up definitions as he goes along, and this is unacceptable in rational discourse. Aren't all intelligent agents

---

6. *God, Evil, and Morality*, 29.
7. *God, Evil, and Morality*, 29.

limited to behave in accordance with their natures? If God's nature includes "perfectly moral" then this means something substantive and meaningful. If he did exist, then he would behave morally 100 percent of the time!

Huffling: "... it is a gross anthropomorphic view of God that holds God is just like us but to an infinite degree. Surely Whittenberger and I do not agree on the existence of God; however, supposing that a creator does exist, there is absolutely no reason to think he is a mirror image of us."[8]

First, all views of gods are anthropomorphic to some degree, and the standard view of God is no exception. All gods are hypothetical intelligent agents, whereas human beings are actual intelligent agents. The gods and human persons belong to the same general class. Secondly, God would not be like human persons to "an infinite degree." Humans have physical bodies, but God would not. Humans are sexual, but God would not be sexual. On the other hand, humans are intelligent, and God would be intelligent to the highest degree. Lastly, to think that God would be a "mirror image" of humans is a straw man, despite Genesis 1:27 which says that God created man in his own image.

Huffling claims that in an investigation of God the only thing we can do is "study the world around us and then make philosophical (*a posteriori*) conclusions about what God is like."[9] The "only thing"? This is mistaken, and I have already shown why. Of course, Huffling could infer from the facts of our world that amoral, apathetic, malicious, and/or sadistic creator gods might exist (i.e., other hypotheses), but these gods would not be God. In fact, the existence of any of these alternative gods would contradict the existence of God. The existence of God would be exclusionary of a competing omnipotent god. There can only be one greatest being.

Huffling: "... if the universe is physical, temporal, and changing, then it would need a cause. But the cause could not have those same characteristics, or we would be led into an infinite regress of causes, which is impossible."[10]

If the universe had no beginning, then the universe would need no cause. The eternal universe idea now has many backers in physics and cosmology, e.g., Steinhardt and Turok.[11] But even if the universe had a beginning and had a cause, this cause need not be a god or God. Also, Huffling

8. *God, Evil, and Morality*, 29.
9. *God, Evil, and Morality*, 30.
10. *God, Evil, and Morality*, 30.
11 Steinhardt and Trick, *Endless Universe*.

has not rationally demonstrated that causes and effects cannot be infinite in time. I don't see why they couldn't be. Religious people already assume an infinite series of causes and effects with respect to the behavior of God.

Huffling (sarcastically): "If we knew exactly what God was like, he wouldn't be much of a God . . . ."[12] This is a straw man. If God did exist, of course we would not know *exactly* what he was like, but he would tell us and show us what he was mostly like.

Huffling: ". . . the more he [God] is not limited like us, the greater he is. The God Whittenberger is describing is more limited than the one I am arguing for."[13]

But ironically, if God did exist, he would be more limited than we are in at least one way and this would make him greater, not lesser, than us. God would be limited in that he would not engage in immoral behavior, whereas we are not limited in this regard and we do engage in immoral behavior. All other things being equal, a god who is limited to behaving morally is more worthy of worship and respect than one not limited in this way, i.e., one who commits both moral and immoral acts.

Huffling: "Whittenberger states that since God is intelligent, he necessarily is moral. There is no logical or metaphysical necessity for such an assertion."[14]

I don't talk about how God is. Rather, I talk about how God would be, if he did exist. God's existence and nature are hypotheses, not realities. However, by the standard definition God would be perfectly moral. Again, Huffling wants to divert our attention from God to his own god, i.e., Huffgod, which he conceives as amoral.

Huffling: "The type of God I am arguing for is a being of infinite existence, and his goodness is not dependent on what he does. He does not achieve goodness like humans do; he is goodness through his very nature of pure being (this is metaphysical, not moral goodness)."[15]

First here, Huffling makes a mistake common among theistic philosophers when he uses the phrase "the type of God I am arguing for . . . ." What he must mean is "the type of *god* I am arguing for," since although there are types of gods, there are no types of God. "God" refers to one unique god, not a type, and we already have a standard definition for this unique god.

12. *God, Evil, and Morality*, 30.
13. *God, Evil, and Morality*, 30.
14. *God, Evil, and Morality*, 31.
15. *God, Evil, and Morality*, 31.

Secondly, "infinite existence" is a vague term and not part of the standard definition. Thirdly, if God did exist, his goodness would be dependent on what he intends, decides, plans, and does, just like the goodness of all intelligent agents depend on these things. And lastly, "metaphysical goodness" is a sham concept. Persons are good with respect to other persons to the extent that they behave morally towards them. The "perfectly moral" attribute of God is more like the "creator" attribute than it is like the "omnipotent" attribute. The former attributes derive from what God would have done, if he did exist, i.e., created a universe and interacted with persons in that universe.

Huffling: "He [Whittenberger] claims that 'all beings or intelligent agents have moral obligations to all other beings.' What I am accused of is saying God *should* be excepted from this rule. However, I am not saying God *should* be excepted . . . I'm saying he *can't* be included."[16]

I believe that "can't be included" is equivalent to "being excepted." If God did exist, then he would be included in the class of "intelligent agents." If all intelligent agents have moral obligations to all other intelligent agents, as I believe they do, then God would have moral obligations to all other intelligent agents, if he did exist. There is no good reason why God would be exempted from this moral principle. Unfortunately, Huffling has bought into the doctrine of divine exceptionalism. He apparently believes that Huffgod or even God would be like a king to which laws, rules, and morals are not applicable. This is an example of special pleading. Also, there is no good reason to think that God would be "outside time" if he did exist. Any act of creation is an act in time.

Huffling implies that I think "God is just a big human." This is just another straw man. Size does not matter. Humans have knowledge, but God would have all possible knowledge. Humans have bodies made of energy-matter, but God would have a body made of some unknown spiritual stuff. Humans have power to do some things, but God would have the power to do all logically possible things. Humans have a gender, but God would have no gender. Humans behave morally some of the time, but God would behave morally all of the time. Humans do not create universes, but God would have created at least one. So, God would not be like humans in some ways, but he would be like humans in other ways but to a greater degree.

Huffling: "'Divine exceptionalism,' he [Whittenberger] says, 'is totally unacceptable to reasonable people.' This is an example of the logical fallacy

---

16. *God, Evil, and Morality*, 31. Emphasis in original.

of poisoning the well. In other words, if one wants to be a reasonable person, then one can't say God is different from other intelligent beings. If one does, then by definition he is not reasonable."[17]

This completely misses the point. Reasonable people are those who have been well trained in the use of reason, the most useful way of thinking. When reasonable people address their skills to the question "To whom do moral rules apply?" they answer "Everyone, of course!" They do not make special pleadings for exceptions as many or most religious persons do. One becomes a reasonable person through education, training, and practice, not through simply agreeing with me.

Huffling: "*Contra* Whittenberger, classical theists don't argue God is 'exempted from objective morality' due to his 'immense power, authority, or creativity'; rather, he is simply not a finite being and is not held to the standards that he imposes on us as finite beings."[18]

Classical theists are just mistaken when they argue this way. Objective morality applies to *all* intelligent agents, not just to finite ones, but also to "infinite" ones, whatever that means. This morality has rules for the way humans should treat each other, the way humans should treat gods, and the way gods should treat humans. This morality is universal. Huffling implies that God would be exempted because he is infinite in some ways. I have heard no good argument for exemptions, and I doubt there are any.

Huffling: "Either we know what God is like (or would be like) or we don't. Further, he [Whittenberger] relies on a mere definition of God to 'prove' that God would be moral."[19]

Either we know what God is like or we don't. True. But going further, we don't know what God is like because God is a *hypothetical*! We don't even know that God exists! If God does not exist, as I have shown, then we could never come to know what he is like. Grabbing the other horn, either we know what God would be like or we don't. True again. But going further with this, we do know what God *would* be like. How? Because we have the standard definition of God which we can use to make rational predictions about what he would and would not do, if he did exist. My four arguments don't prove that God would be moral, as Huffling claims. They weren't intended to do that. Rather, the standard definition of God stipulates that God would be perfectly moral. I just look at the implications of that. My

17. *God, Evil, and Morality*, 31–32.
18. *God, Evil, and Morality*, 32.
19. *God, Evil, and Morality*, 32.

four arguments prove that God, as defined in the standard manner, does not exist!

Huffling: "My point is that (natural) science studies nature. We can certainly infer God (through philosophy); however, that moves away from nature to the supernatural."[20]

Science studies reality, not just nature. "Nature" is a concept invented in the course of studying reality with science. Huffling talks as if "the supernatural" is some part of reality, but so far, neither he nor anybody else has provided any good evidence to show beyond a reasonable doubt that anything "supernatural" actually exists. As far as we know so far, there appear to be no supernatural things, objects, beings, events, or realms. If God did exist, then he would have created and would have interacted with our world and this would be detectable with science. If a god did exist and did not create our world and did not interact with it, then he would be of no interest to us.

I presented an argument against the existence of God based on prayer. In response Huffling said "I will just say that even granting such a position on prayer does not logically necessitate God's non-existence."[21] Yes, it does! The premises of my argument are true and the logic is valid, and so the conclusion must be true—God does not exist. Huffling doesn't like it, but he has shown no error in this argument.

Huffling: "To break a rule of reason is to violate a law of logic."[22]

Breaking rules of reason includes violating laws of logic but is not identical with it. In the case we are discussing, Huffling and other Christians break the rule of reason "Don't change a definition simply because you don't like a conclusion rationally reached through the use of it." What they have done and continue to do is change the definition of 'God' after it has been shown that God does not exist. Contrary to Huffling, the standard definition of 'God' includes the attribute "perfectly moral," not the attribute "amoral."

Huffling: "In the end, God's existence is a question of philosophy, not natural science."[23]

---

20. *God, Evil, and Morality*, 33.
21. *God, Evil, and Morality*, 33.
22. *God, Evil, and Morality*, 33.
23. *God, Evil, and Morality*, 33.

I disagree. God's existence is a question of philosophy, science, and even history. All these disciplines can be, are, and should be used to tackle the question.

Huffling: "Unfortunately, there is no philosophical reasoning provided by Whittenberger for God being moral; merely an *a priori* definition of God that says God is moral from which the conclusion is drawn that God is moral and would not allow evil."[24]

This description is partly correct. I do start with the standard definition of God which stipulates that the hypothetical God is perfectly moral, not partly moral or amoral. There's nothing wrong with using an "*a priori*" definition like this. With this definition I rationally predict what we should observe and not observe in this world with respect to the Great Tsunami, the Holocaust, men who rape women, and the effects of prayer. These predictions are disconfirmed. And thus, God does not exist. In contrast, Huffling assumes that Huffgod is amoral. For now, I won't attempt to generalize my arguments from God to Huffgod. We might broach that topic after Huffling finally agrees with me that God does not exist.

---

24. *God, Evil, and Morality*, 33.

6

Rejecting the Standard Definition While Offering Arguments for God

J. Brian Huffling

In the previous chapter it was argued that God does not exist due to the problem of evil. The problem of evil is used to show that God would have moral obligations to prevent at least certain types of evil from occurring, and since such evils occur, then God does not exist. I have argued that God is not a moral being and thus has no moral obligation, thereby deflating the alleged problem of evil. While Whittenberger wants to define God *a priori* based on a mere definition, I think this is the wrong way to go about discovering what God is. (To satisfy Whittenberger's point, when I say something like "what God is," it is noted that "is" means "would be" for an atheist.) I think it is odd for one who wants to make arguments from science to go about the question of God's existence in a non-scientific way.

Scientists make conclusions based on observation, which is necessarily *a posteriori*; however, Whittenberger wants to discuss God's existence in an *a priori* fashion apart from any experience or observation, i.e., without experiencing or observing the world. This could be because, as an atheist, he does not think we can reason from experience to a God who is not there. However, history is littered with philosophers and scientists who make such cosmological, *demonstratia quia* arguments, i.e., from effect (universe) to cause (God). While I will get into theistic proofs in more detail later, it is enough to show that if the universe is contingent and cannot account for its own existence, it needs a cause that is not identical to it. If there is such a cause, then it would have a radically different nature than finite, contingent human beings. Whereas we would be material, finite, changing, temporal, etc., the cause of such qualities could not have those qualities, since such qualities are inherently part of contingent being and thus require a cause. *Contra* Whittenberger, there cannot be an infinite regress of causes (as shown from many philosophers, such as Aristotle); thus, there must be a cause that has no such contingent qualities, an uncaused cause. It would be incumbent on us to *discover* what this cause (God) is like rather than to *stipulate* (a word Whittenberger uses to describe his own position) what he is like.

Opposed to this scientific exploration of God, Whittenberger wants to work from a "standard definition." He admits he is not arguing for this position but is merely positing God via this definition that stuck.[1] There are several problems with such a method. First, he does not say where he is getting this definition, only that it is generally accepted.

Second, as he even admits, there is more than one definition of God used even in theistic circles (even in Christianity) throughout history.[2] It is instructive to note the words of Ronald Nash: "Much recent philosophical and theological literature reflects the struggle between two competing concepts of God."[3] These two views are classical theism and process theology. This demonstrates there is no reigning definition.

Third, if there is a standard definition, it probably follows the orthodox position of Augustine, Anselm, and Aquinas. But this causes a problem since several of the attributes Whittenberger says are part of the standard definition really aren't. For example, he says being perfectly moral is *ipso facto* part of this definition (with absolutely no citations to support it). I would argue that a close examination of the above thinkers as well as the rest of the church fathers would actually reveal that they did not see God having a moral nature in the sense that Whittenberger says he does. Further, Whittenberger says that God would have to be moral since he would know how he should behave based on some standard. But where would such a standard come from? If it "existed" apart from God then God could only be good, according to Whittenberger, by behaving in accordance with said standard. But this raises a serious problem for the standard definition:

1. *God, Evil, and Morality*, 36.
2. *God, Evil, and Morality*, 36.
3. Nash, *The Concept of God*, 19.

if God's goodness and knowledge are dependent on some standard that is apart from God, then he does not exist *a se* (completely on his own, independently from anything else). However, whatever definition we use of God in the classical sense (putting aside process theology, etc.), divine aseity is most assuredly part of that definition, in fact, it is an essential doctrine. But if God somehow depends on something else, then he can't be *a se*. This raises a logical contradiction for Whittenberger: God can only be moral by adhering to some "external standard" (adhering to himself as his own standard is incoherent and reduces to complete divine voluntarism, which would also defeat Whittenberger's position), which denies his aseity. But to deny his aseity is to deny the standard definition (by any classical account). Thus, to maintain that God is beholden to some standard other than himself violates the standard definition. Further, Whittenberger says that "'infinite existence' is a vague term and not part of the standard definition."[4] What "infinite" means may be disputed, but no classical theist can maintain that God is not infinite. It is most assuredly part of the standard (classical) definition. Last, he says that "there is no good reason to think that God would be 'outside time' if he did exist." This is debatable, especially in today's theological milieu where almost everything is debated about God's nature, even in evangelical circles (a clear demonstration that we can't just define God and leave it at that). However, if we are using the *standard* bearers of orthodoxy throughout the early church and Middle Ages, such as Augustine, Anselm, Aquinas, and pretty much anyone until very recently, then it is most certainly the case that being "outside time" *is* part of the standard definition. Further, creation being "an act *in* time" is outside of the classical view as well. Whittenberger will have to concede such attributes unless he wants to dispute the definition; however, I don't see on what grounds he can do so without trying to argue for what God would be like *apart* from the standard definition.

Fourth, as just noted, even in evangelical circles there is great debate on almost all the attributes of God and what they mean. No one settles for a mere definition of God; rather, philosophers and theologians try to *discover* via perfect being theology (in an *a priori* way *a la* Anselm) or through a *demonstratia quia* way (an *a posteriori* approach *a la* Aquinas) what God is like.

Fifth, simply defining God this way begs the question in favor of one view. Such positions must be demonstrated not stipulated. Not only that,

---

4. *God, Evil, and Morality*, 40.

but it has to be clarified. What does it mean for God to be morally perfect? I have presented arguments for why God is not moral, and Whittenberger has chosen to ignore those arguments. However, if I am correct, then the problem raised by Shermer and Whittenberger fails. It is thus incumbent on Whittenberger to refute my reasoning for why God is not moral.

Sixth, even granting that God is a morally perfect being, there has been no demonstration that by allowing suffering or harm that God is necessarily breaking some moral precept. The three great theistic religions, Judaism, Christianity, and Islam, all grant that God allows suffering yet there is no worry that God is somehow morally bad because of it. Even Job in the end repents for thinking God is unjust. It is at least *conceivable* that what it means for a transcendent, creator-God to be morally perfect is not what it means for a creature to be so.

A question I would ask Whittenberger is: what are these universal standards that God is beholden to and where do they come from? Given classical theism, God is the cause of all things that exist (other than himself, as God has no cause). Thus, there would be nothing else that is eternal and uncaused besides God. I am arguing that no such standards that transcend God "exist." What would it mean for them to exist? Such principles are wholly obscure, unclear, and unexplained. They are at best debated, but again, not stipulated.

On a similar note, it is not clear what Whittenberger thinks about human morality. It seems that he holds to natural evolution, so what moral theory does he subscribe to? Is morality objective? It's hard to see how it could be on an evolutionary view since humans would simply be the product of chance. There is nothing transcendent to give humans any more worth than any other animal. On a theistic view, humans have a nature which includes a *telos*, or goal. In other words, a way humans are *supposed* to behave. But there is no way humans are *supposed* to behave on a simply evolutionary view (other than for egoistic or utilitarian reasons, but even these could not really be objective apart from a human *telos*). Even if morality is the product of evolution, in what sense would this apply to God who has not undergone evolution?

Regarding morality, Whittenberger wants to define evil in terms of *harm*.[5] But why is harm bad or evil? There has to be a reason why harm is bad. Harming a biological being simply describes the state of such beings. But the fact that a being is harmed does not tell us why it *shouldn't*

---

5. *God, Evil, and Morality*, 35.

be harmed. Whittenberger is reducing the notion of evil to materialism. However, the notion of evil is inherently philosophical. Many philosophers define evil as a corruption of a good thing. But such a corruption is tied to what a thing should be. This has to do with, in our case, human nature. But the nature of humans, what they are and what they should be, is inherently philosophical. If we are going to have a discussion on evil, we have to do so in the realm of philosophy and not reduce evil to materialism. Of course, there are different kinds of evil, such as physical evil (e.g., destruction or *harm* from natural disasters). But there is also moral evil. It seems that God would be committing moral evil, according to Whittenberger. Humans also commit moral evil. But moral evil cannot be reduced to mere physical things. In order to say humans (or God) *shouldn't* behave in such and such a way, we have to know how they should act. But such is no mere materialist enterprise and simply saying that humans do x, therefore they *should* do x commits the is/ought fallacy. In other words, morality is not a physical property. The only way to say humans should behave in such a way that offers a transcendent explanation must rise above materialistic reductionism.

At the heart of Whittenberger's last chapter is his notion that God is a moral being and that I am inventing a lesser god.[6] He argues that he does not have "to demonstrate that God is a perfectly moral being." He states, "Most religious people *assume* this is the case, and I am simply running with their assumption. My obligation is just to rationally demonstrate that God does not exist, and that is exactly what I have done."[7] I would agree that at least many *present* religious people *assume* God is a moral being. However, in a debate, we can't simply assume our position. We have to demonstrate it. As I said in a previous chapter, if Whittenberger were having a debate on a point in psychology, he could not simply assume his position. He would have to demonstrate it. That is especially the case if we are talking about a central tenet of the debate. We can't simply run "with their assumption." There are plenty of theologians and philosophers who don't hold that God is a moral being, such as Herbert McCabe and Brian Davies. It can also be argued that such was the orthodox position throughout the centuries and the view that God is moral in the way Whittenberger and others are saying is a new view. In any event, given that respected theologians and philosophers reject the notion that God is a moral being (and that such might be a

---

6. *God, Evil, and Morality*, 36.
7. *God, Evil, and Morality*, 36. Emphasis added.

more foreign view than many realize), we cannot simply run with a certain group's assumptions while ignoring the other side of the debate.

Whittenberger says God and humans are in the same class of beings.[8] Classically, this is not the case as there is a sharp creator/creature distinction due to the different natures of God and humans. Even the concept "intelligent" is applied analogously between God and creatures as they don't "reason" the same way.

Further, I am going to argue that Whittenberger has in fact not rationally demonstrated that God doesn't exist. He has made several versions of the harm principle that stipulates that if God did exist, he would not let evil things happen; but, since they do happen, God must not exist. The first premise in his various arguments are stipulations that are not defended in any way but merely assumed. It is this assumption that I'm calling into question.

Regarding Whittenberger's argument from prayer, the first premise assumes what God would do. There is no reason to think that God would necessarily "favorably respond to intercessory prayers for healing."[9] There is no demonstration or support for this crucial premise. It is also important to mention the Bible does not teach this. Nowhere does it say that God will or must respond favorably to prayer. There are passages that teach God heals, but it is never taken that he *must* do so. Such does not disprove God's existence. God can logically exist and not answer prayer. Again, we need demonstration, not stipulation.

One of the responses to the problem of evil is what Brian Davies calls the "We already know God exists" argument.[10] This means that if there are positive proofs for God, then evil won't negate those arguments. For example, if the universe requires a cause, then the "existence" of evil and suffering does not negate that need for a cause. Let's look at some of the positive reasons for God's existence.

Since I have argued that God's existence is a philosophical question, I am going to focus on the philosophical arguments, and in particular, the cosmological arguments. I will summarize the first couple of Aquinas' five ways and the kalam argument. All of these arguments have two aspects in common: the universe cannot account for its own existence and an actual infinity of causes is impossible.

---

8. *God, Evil, and Morality*, 38.
9. *God, Evil, and Morality*, 24.
10. Davies, *The Reality of God*, 17.

The first way is an argument from change—Aquinas uses the word "motion" in the sense defined by Aristotle; in fact, the argument for an uncaused cause originated with Aristotle. (This is a point worth making: while atheists, especially those who follow the new atheism, want to argue that arguments for God's existence are based on the fancies of religious people who can't think well, the fact is that the history of ideas is replete with the world's greatest thinkers like Aristotle and Aquinas who had sophisticated arguments for theism.) Aquinas says the following: it is evident that things around us change. What he means by a change is when something goes from potentially being something to actually being something. Act and potency are *principles of being* in Aristotelian and Thomistic metaphysics. Act is when something is *actually* in some state of existence while *potency* is the possibility for that thing to change or exist. But a change can only be brought about by something that is already in act. Furthermore, nothing can bring itself into act. Things cannot be in act and potency in the same respect simultaneously. The example Aquinas uses is wood being made hot. Before being hot it is in potency to being hot. The fire, which is actually hot, brings the wood into actually being hot. A key point is that a thing cannot simultaneously be the mover and the thing that is moved—that would require a thing being in act and potency in the same respect simultaneously, which is a contradiction. What is moved, or changed, has to be changed by something else, even if that something else is itself changed by something else, and so on. But this can't go on forever. Such would mean there would be no first mover or first movement (change), or any subsequent change. But there is such change. Thus, there must be a being that is not composed of different parts like act and potency. Since act is *being* and potency is in itself not a thing, this being would be what Aristotle (and Aquinas) called Pure Act. This is a being that is not limited in any way. As Aquinas says, all men know this being to be God.

If this argument is sound, it not only tells us that God exists, but it tells us a lot about his nature and attributes. There are some misunderstandings with this argument, such as the objection that Newton's laws refute it since objects that are in motion or rest stay in such a state until impeded. However, Newton's laws are laws of *physics* while the notion of change in this context is *metaphysical*. Aquinas is talking about change, not inertia. Further, the "who created God?" objection does not touch this argument if it is sound since God would be an *uncaused* being. Another misunderstanding appears when one objects that I can cause the change in my body when

I move my hand. However, the hand is not ultimately moving itself: the nerves firing from the brain to the hand cause the movement. Ultimately (except in involuntary cases) the will is the cause of this change, which receives its being, along with the person's being, from the ultimate cause. In any event, the "self-motion" in this objection does not defeat Aquinas' point.

The next way, according to Aquinas, is the argument from efficient causality. It is very similar to the first way but different in that instead of arguing about change, it argues that a thing cannot be the cause of its existence. This is because it would have to exist in order to bring itself into existence, which is a contradiction. One thing causing another in this way cannot go to infinity since if the efficient cause (the thing that brings something else into being or affects something else) were part of an infinite chain of causes, there would be no first cause. But if there is no first cause, there would be no intermediary causes either, and no ultimate effect. Since there are effects, there must be a finite number of efficient causes, with one ultimate efficient cause, of which men call God.

An example of this argument is a train. (I owe this example to Richard Howe.) If one asks what is pulling a certain boxcar, it is legitimate for the answer to be, the boxcar in front of it. But this kind of explanation can't go on forever; there must be an engine. The basic thrust of this argument is that finite things cannot account for their own existence, and we cannot make an infinite series of causes to explain the existence of finite things. Thus, there must be an ultimate cause that is itself not caused, i.e., an uncaused cause. The fact that this being is uncaused heads off the objection "who created God?"

The point of all of this (which is similar to the third way of Aquinas) is that things we experience in the universe cannot account for their own existence. They are contingent. But one contingent thing giving rise to another cannot go backwards to infinity. Thus, there must be a necessary being to account for contingent existence. In short, as Norman Geisler used to say, since something exists, something must have always existed.[11] If there was ever a "time" when nothing existed, then nothing ever would exist. Since things do exist, something must have always existed. It can't be the universe, so it must be a transcendent being.

Why can't the universe just be? Because it is contingent, changing, and had a beginning. Such things cannot account for their own existence. Given

---

11. Geisler, *Christian Apologetics*, 265–71 (Kindle).

that the universe came to be about 13.7 billion years ago, "before" that there was no universe.

Regarding the proposal that the universe has an infinite past, let's look at the kalam argument. It was first argued by Islamic philosophers to say that (1) An actual infinite can't exist; (2) an infinite succession of past moments would be an actual infinite; therefore, (3) there can't be an infinite succession of past moments. In other words, the universe must be temporally finite. The argument has been modernized by William Lane Craig's use of Big Bang cosmology. This version says: (1) Everything that has a beginning has a cause; (2) the universe had a beginning; therefore, (3) the universe had a cause. Virtual particles are often offered as a counterexample to premise (1) since they are said to pop into existence via nothing. However, virtual particles arise from unstable energy in a vacuum. Since unstable energy is not nothing, virtual particles are not a counterexample. The objection, "who created God?" doesn't get off the ground since the argument says that things *that have a beginning* must have a cause. Since God is argued to be a being with no beginning, this objection fails.

The evidence for the second premise is Big Bang cosmology. For example, the second law of thermodynamics states that usable energy is running out and if the universe were infinitely old it would have run out by now. The expansion of the universe shows that if time were reversed the universe would collapse back into nothing. The radiation echo discovered in the 1960s demonstrates there was a massive explosion that led to the expansion of the universe. As agnostic Anthony Kenny said, "A proponent of such a theory, at least if he is an atheist, must believe that the matter of the universe came from nothing and by nothing."[12]

Such is the reigning theory in astrophysics and cosmology. The various kalam-style arguments are predicated on the temporal finitude of the universe; however, the Thomistic arguments are not and would still be valid even if the universe were temporally infinite. This is because it is not the impossibility of an infinity of *temporal* moments that Aquinas has a problem with (although I disagree with him and think this is a problem); his point was that even given such a scenario, there cannot be an infinite *hierarchy* of causes. Thus, while he allowed for a possible infinity of *per accidens* causes, he did not allow for *per se* causes to be infinite. *Per accidens* causes would be like a father having a son and that son having a son. There is no logical problem (in Aquinas' view) for such an infinite series; however, a *per*

---

12. Kenny, *Studies in Ethics*, 66 (Kindle).

se ordered series of efficient causes, such as a hand moving a stick which moves a stone, could not be infinite.

In conclusion, I have provided several philosophical arguments that God exists. These arguments must be analyzed and evaluated on their own terms. In other words, in order to reject them, one must refute them. In order to refute them, one must show that they are either invalid or unsound. I want to point out again that the question of God's existence is a philosophical question. In order to settle it one way or the other, we must do philosophy. It will not do to claim that science has disproven God. Science is not the sort of thing that could do that (as mentioned earlier and agreed with by Shermer). It will also not do to merely take rhetorical swipes at the above arguments. One must provide a philosophical analysis.

7

Correct Universal Ethics and God's Moral Standing

GARY J. WHITTENBERGER

IN RESPONDING TO HUFFLING'S Chapter 6, I will do what I did previously—simply comment on what I believe to be my opponent's most germane quotes.

Huffling: "While Whittenberger wants to define God *a priori* based on a mere definition, I think this is the wrong way to go about discovering what God is."[1]

If God does not exist, then it is impossible to discover "what God is." Huffling is begging the question "Does God exist?" and this is not allowed in standard philosophical investigation. The right way to begin is to use the standard definition of "God" which I presented and proceed from there. Definitions are not "mere." They are extremely important in philosophical and scientific discourse.

Huffling: "While I will get into theistic proofs in more detail later, it is enough to show that if the universe is contingent and cannot account for its own existence, it needs a cause that is not identical to it. If there is such a cause, then it would have a radically different nature than finite, contingent human beings."[2]

---

1. *God, Evil, and Morality*, 44.
2. *God, Evil, and Morality*, 44–45.

If my arguments against the existence of God are sound, and they are, then it will do no good for Huffling to present theistic proofs. He would be wasting his time. Nevertheless, on the tangential topic of cosmology it appears that Huffling ignored the comments I made in my last chapter. If the universe is not contingent, i.e., if it has always existed, then it does account for its own existence and no cause of it is needed. Furthermore, even if it were contingent, there are no good reasons to think that its cause would have a "radically different nature" from plain old energy-matter. Ockham's Razor requires that we not multiply assumptions beyond necessity.

Huffling: "*Contra* Whittenberger, there cannot be an infinite regress of causes (as shown from many philosophers, such as Aristotle); thus, there would be a cause that has no such contingent qualities."[3]

Here again Huffling is going off on a tangent. Neither he, Aristotle, nor anybody else has *shown* that there cannot be an infinite regress of causes. If the universe is simply the totality of dynamic-orderly energy-matter in space-time which has always existed, then there could be an infinite regress of causes and effects intrinsic to the universe without any external cause of the universe.

Huffling: "First, he [Whittenberger] does not say where he is getting this definition, only that it is generally accepted."[4]

The standard definition of "God," for which I presented a short version, comes from a distillation of scriptures of the Abrahamic religions, the writings of theologians and philosophers of religion, dictionaries, sermons of religious leaders, and discussions with, writings from, and surveys of lay persons, over roughly the last three thousand years. So far, Huffling has objected to only one component of this standard definition. I claimed that God is conceived as perfectly moral, but he claimed that God is conceived as amoral. I believe he is mistaken. I challenge him to ask a random sample of people shopping at a public mall what they think on this issue. I am confident that most will see it as I do.

Huffling: "It is instructive to note the words of Ronald Nash: 'Much recent philosophical and theological literature reflects the struggle between two competing concepts of God.'"[5]

Surely there have been many competing concepts of God, but this does not negate the fact that there is now a standard definition of God

---

3. *God, Evil, and Morality*, 45.
4. *God, Evil, and Morality*, 45.
5. *God, Evil, and Morality*, 45.

which would be endorsed by billions of lay persons and by thousands of philosophers of religion throughout the world, if we were to take a proper survey. Although I have not yet challenged the existence of other gods, like Huffgod, I have shown that God does not exist.

Huffling: "I would argue that a close examination of the above thinkers [Augustine, Anselm, and Aquinas] as well as the rest of the church fathers would actually reveal that they did not see God having a moral nature in the sense that Whittenberger says he does."[6]

The last of these named thinkers, i.e., Aquinas, died 746 years ago! So, I do not think we should expect the definitions of "God" of these three men to measure up to the modern standard definition which I have presented. Furthermore, Huffling has not shown how any of these thinkers thought of God as having a moral nature different from the sense I outlined.

Huffling: "Further, Whittenberger says that God would have to be moral since he would know how he should behave based on some standard. But where would such a standard come from?"[7]

Good question! By thinking rationally God would have created the moral standard before he created other persons. I have called this standard "correct universal ethics" or "CUE," which would specify how persons should and should not treat one another. Henceforth, God would behave in accordance with CUE and expect other persons to do likewise.

Huffling: "However, whatever definition we use of God in the classical sense (putting aside process theology, etc.), divine aseity is most assuredly part of that definition, in fact, it is an essential doctrine."[8]

When Huffling refers to "God in the classical sense," he is actually referring to the standard definition which I have summarized. According to one respected source, "Aseity, as a divine attribute, refers to God's self-existence. In other words, God is not dependent upon anything else for his existence but has eternally existed without any external or prior cause."[9] I agree with Huffling that aseity is a property of God, according to the standard definition. I did not include it in the short version of the definition because I did not think it was relevant to the particular arguments against God's existence on which we are focused.

---

6. *God, Evil, and Morality*, 45.
7. *God, Evil, and Morality*, 45.
8. *God, Evil, and Morality*, 46.
9. Grenz, Guretzki, and Nordling, *Pocket Dictionary*, 16.

Huffling: "But to deny his aseity is to deny the standard definition (by any classical account). Thus, to maintain that God is beholden to some standard other than himself violates the standard definition."[10]

God would be beholden to a moral standard *which he created*, and thus I am not denying aseity. There is no violation of the standard definition.

Huffling: "What 'infinite' means may be disputed, but no classical theist can maintain that God is not infinite."[11]

"Infinite" does not stand by itself. It must be presented in reference to some feature, trait, property, or attribute. So, one might say that God is infinitely old, but not that God is infinitely sadistic. I suppose we could say that God is infinitely moral, but that formulation is awkward and unclear. The term "perfectly moral" is much better. Although the short version of the standard definition that I have presented does not include the word "infinite" or its derivatives, it does imply that some of God's traits are indeed infinite. A good example is "all-powerful."

Huffling: "However, if we are using the *standard* bearers of orthodoxy ... then it is most certainly the case that being 'outside time' *is* part of the standard definition. Further, creation being 'an act *in* time' is outside of the classical view."[12]

I'm not willing to allow Huffling to cherry pick the "standard bearers of orthodoxy." The standard definition of God is based on the modal view of all the bearers of orthodoxy over the millennia, especially common folk. I believe Augustine's view was that God existed "outside time," but this idea is nonsensical. If God did exist, then he would have engaged in a succession of acts, and thus exist in time.

Huffling: "What does it mean for God to be morally perfect?"[13]

To be precise, I used the term "perfectly moral." It means that God would always conform to CUE which he invented before he created other persons.

Huffling: "I have presented arguments for why God is not moral. . . . It is thus incumbent on Whittenberger to refute my reasoning for why God is not moral."[14]

---

10. *God, Evil, and Morality*, 46.
11. *God, Evil, and Morality*, 46.
12. *God, Evil, and Morality*, 46. Emphasis in original.
13. *God, Evil, and Morality*, 47.
14. *God, Evil, and Morality*, 47.

Huffling has presented no arguments in this regard and so there are none to refute. Just as I have stipulated that God is perfectly moral by definition, Huffling has similarly stipulated that God is amoral. However, he is defining a different god, which I have named "Huffgod." I have only proven that God does not exist, not yet that Huffgod does not exist. That might take another debate or book.

Huffling: "... even granting that God is a morally perfect being, there has been no demonstration that by allowing suffering or harm that God is necessarily breaking some moral precept."[15]

I am pleased to make the demonstration now. The relevant moral rule in this case can be formulated this way: "Person X should prevent harm to person Y, if he is able, unless allowing the harm is necessary for producing a greater gain and X also justifies this exception." This moral rule, which I will label "MR#1," is applicable in this argument which I presented earlier:

1. If God did exist, then the Great Southeast Asia Tsunami of December 2004 would not have occurred.
2. The Great Southeast Asia Tsunami of December 2004 did occur.
3. Therefore, God does not exist.

MR#1 is the necessary background for the truth of the first premise in the argument. If God did exist, then he would always follow all moral rules of CUE, including MR#1. If he had followed this rule with respect to the tsunami, then it would not have occurred. God would have been able to prevent it because he would be all-powerful. Allowing the tsunami would not have been necessary for producing a greater gain because God would be an all-powerful creator for whom no particular event or contingency in the world is necessary. And nobody, including God, presented any justification for the tsunami before, during, or after its occurrence. Thus, by following the logic we see that God does not exist.

Huffling: "It is at least *conceivable* that what it means for a transcendent, creator-God to be morally perfect is not what it means for a creature to be so."[16]

It is possible to claim this, but it is not rational to do so. CUE applies to all persons. Human beings are persons, and if God did exist, he would be a person too! Any person is perfectly moral if he is compliant with CUE

---

15. *God, Evil, and Morality*, 47.
16. *God, Evil, and Morality*, 47.

100 percent of the time. Huffling is engaged in special pleading for God, and this is a logical fallacy. Again, he is desperately clinging to the doctrine of divine exceptionalism, like a Titanic survivor clinging to a wooden scrap in the frigid Atlantic.

Huffling: "Such [moral] principles are wholly obscure, unclear, and unexplained. They are at best debated, but again, not stipulated."[17]

Here Huffling contradicts what he said in chapter 2 when he spoke of himself and Shermer: "we both believe, albeit for different reasons, that morality is something known rather intuitively.... we both take morality to be objective."[18] He can't have it both ways! When Huffling talks of objective morality and I talk of CUE, I believe we are pointing to the same thing. The moral rules of CUE have been stipulated by wise men and women, philosophers of ethics, and theologians over the millennia, but yes, they have yet to be collected and codified in one document. A better project would be to challenge a panel of moral experts to devise CUE "from scratch" by thinking rationally, as God would have done, if he existed.

Huffling: "... it is not clear what Whittenberger thinks about human morality."[19]

Actually, it should be fairly clear by now. I believe in one morality for all persons, whether they be human, divine, alien, or robotic persons, with no exceptions. This morality, which I call "correct universal ethics" (CUE), is devised by rational thinking. If God did exist, he would have been the first to devise CUE. However, even persons confined to planets can at least approximate CUE if they think rationally about different social interactions. It is not clear what Huffling thinks about morality.

Huffling: "Regarding morality, Whittenberger wants to define evil in terms of *harm*. But why is harm bad or evil? There has to be a reason why harm is bad."[20]

That's not quite accurate. I have no interest in the term "evil." I think it is a confusing term with a religious basis, now obsolete. We have no need of it. I think morality can be defined mostly in terms of rules regarding harms and benefits resulting from interactions of persons. "Why is harm bad?" That seems to be a rather silly question, but maybe I am missing something. I think everyone would agree that harm is bad, a condition to be prevented,

17. *God, Evil, and Morality*, 47.
18. *God, Evil, and Morality*, 11.
19. *God, Evil, and Morality*, 47.
20. *God, Evil, and Morality*, 47. Emphasis in original.

delayed, terminated, shortened, or reduced. I don't necessarily think there has to be a reason why harm is bad. Does there have to be a reason for all facts? Does there have to be a reason why electrons exist? Is it possible that they just do? If God did exist, would there have to be a reason why he exists?

Huffling: "I would agree that at least many *present* religious people *assume* God is a moral being. However, in a debate, we can't simply assume our position. We have to demonstrate it."[21]

Since Huffling and I agree that many people conceive of God as a moral being, I don't see why we need to demonstrate this point of our agreement. We might quibble about the percentage of human persons who have this view. I predict that if we did a proper survey we would find that at least 90 percent of all the people who say they believe in God would agree with this statement: "God is perfectly moral." Huffling would likely make a different prediction, but it doesn't really matter. For the billions of persons who hold to the standard conception and believe that God does exist, I and others have shown that God in fact does not exist! I doubt we will have time or space to address the existence of Huffgod.

Huffling: "Even the concept 'intelligent' is applied analogously between God and creatures as they don't 'reason' the same way."[22]

We know that human persons exist and we can describe them with concepts such as 'intelligent' and 'reasoning.' Neither Huffling nor anybody else knows that God exists. Again, as I have said before, God is just a hypothetical. By the standard definition, God is an intelligent and reasoning being. I am just generalizing well-founded concepts from humans to God, and there is nothing wrong with that. Does Huffling think that if God did exist he would not use the rules of logic that we use? Does Huffling think that if God did exist he would not make rational inferences from evidence, as we do when we think efficiently?

Huffling: "The first premise in his various arguments are stipulations that are not defended in any way but merely assumed. It is this assumption that I'm calling into question."[23]

I am pleased to wipe away this doubt. For example, let's take this first premise: "1. If God did exist, then the Great Southeast Asia Tsunami of December 2004 would not have occurred." Why? By definition, if God did exist, he would be all-powerful and perfectly moral. If a person is perfectly

---

21. *God, Evil, and Morality*, 48. Emphasis in original.
22. *God, Evil, and Morality*, 49.
23. *God, Evil, and Morality*, 49.

moral, then he conforms to all moral rules of CUE 100 percent of the time. MR#1 of CUE requires prevention of harm under specific conditions. The prevention by God of a disaster from a tsunami would meet these conditions. Therefore, God would have prevented the Great Tsunami and it would not have occurred. The other first premises are justified in a similar manner.

Huffling: "Regarding Whittenberger's argument from prayer, the first premise assumes what God would do. There is no reason to think that God would necessarily 'favorably respond to intercessory prayers for healing.'"[24]

But there are two good reasons to think that God would necessarily respond this way: God would be all-powerful and he would be perfectly moral. Powerful and moral persons heal when they can, and especially when they are asked. If Huffling himself already possessed a vaccine for the coronavirus now plaguing humanity would he administer it to persons who asked for help? He would, if he were a moral person. If God did exist, he would do no less in many similar situations.

Huffling: "Nowhere [in the Bible] does it say that God will or must respond favorably to prayer."[25]

Huffling's claim here is soundly refuted by the following verses:
"And I will do whatever you ask in my name, so that the Father may be glorified in the Son" (John 14:13). "Therefore I tell you, whatever you ask for in prayer, believe that you have received it, and it will be yours" (Mark 11:24). "But when you pray, go into your room, close the door and pray to your Father, who is unseen. Then your Father, who sees what is done in secret, will reward you" (Matt 6:6). "Again, truly I tell you that if two of you on earth agree about anything they ask for, it will be done for them by my Father in heaven" (Matt 18:19). "Is anyone among you sick? Let them call the elders of the church to pray over them and anoint them with oil in the name of the Lord. And the prayer offered in faith will make the sick person well; the Lord will raise them up" (Jas 5:14–15). "So I say to you: Ask and it will be given to you; seek and you will find; knock and the door will be opened to you. For everyone who asks receives; the one who seeks finds; and to the one who knocks, the door will be opened" (Luke 11:9–10).

Huffling: "God can logically exist and not answer prayer."[26]

24. *God, Evil, and Morality*, 49.
25. *God, Evil, and Morality*, 49.
26. *God, Evil, and Morality*, 49.

It is logically impossible for God to exist and not favorably intervene in response to a request for healing. The reasons are the same—God would be all-powerful and he would be perfectly moral and thus comply with MR#1. Demonstration provided.

Huffling: "This means that if there are positive proofs for God, then evil won't negate those arguments."[27]

If any one of my four arguments against God's existence is correct, then other arguments presented in favor of God's existence must be flawed and incorrect. Neither Huffling nor anyone else has rationally demonstrated that my premises are false or that my logic is invalid. Therefore, at least for now, my conclusion stands—God does not exist.

Huffling, channeling Aquinas: "What is moved, or changed, has to be changed by something else, even if that something else is itself changed by something else, and so on. But this can't go on forever."[28]

The first claim here is a tautology and has no value. Even if there were some first mover, it would not need to be any god or God.

Huffling: "Further, the 'who created God?' objection does not touch this argument [from Aquinas] if it is sound since God would be an *uncaused* being."[29]

In the standard definition, God is eternal and thus nothing would have caused God to come into existence. But I have shown that God does not exist.

Huffling, still channeling Aquinas: "But if there is no first cause, there would be no intermediary causes either, and no ultimate effect. Since there are effects, there must be a finite number of efficient causes, with one ultimate efficient cause, of which men call God."[30]

There could be either a finite or an infinite chain of causes and effects. We don't know which is the case. But even if the former were the case and there was one ultimate efficient cause, it need not be a god or God.

Huffling, paraphrasing Howe: "An example of this argument is a train. . . . If one asks what is pulling a certain boxcar, it is legitimate for the answer to be, the boxcar in front of it. But this can't go on forever; there must be an engine."[31]

27. *God, Evil, and Morality*, 49.
28. *God, Evil, and Morality*, 50.
29. *God, Evil, and Morality*, 50. Emphasis in original.
30. *God, Evil, and Morality*, 51.
31. *God, Evil, and Morality*, 51.

A counterexample is a universe filled with small particles with them moving, remaining stationary, combining, disassociating, and/or colliding, forever. Imagine a universe in which order and change are just inherent and eternal features for small particles. It is easy to do. This is a better model of the universe than the train analogy.

Huffling: "Thus, there must be a necessary being to account for contingent existence."[32]

The term "being" here is ambiguous; it has two different meanings. It can mean "any thing that exists" or "any intelligent thing that exists." I agree that there must be at least one thing that necessarily exists, but this need not be an *intelligent* thing. Also, if the particle model of the universe is correct, then the set of necessary, noncontingent things is probably infinite. Combinations and disassociations can account for the contingent existence of different things. For example, a baby owes its contingent existence to the combining of atoms in a unique way.

Huffling: "Why can't the universe just be? Because it is contingent, changing, and had a beginning. Given that the universe came to be about 13.7 billion years ago, 'before' that there was no universe."[33]

But the universe can just be! The evidence conclusively supports only one of Huffling's three claims here. The universe is changing; that is true. But the evidence we have so far is insufficient to conclude that the universe is contingent and that it had a beginning. The Big Bang did occur about 13.7 billion years ago, but this is best explained as a transition event rather than a creation *ex nihilo*.

Huffling: The [kalam] argument has been modernized by William Lane Craig's use of Big Bang cosmology. This version says: . . . (2) The universe had a beginning . . ."[34]

Craig's argument fails because the facts of physics and cosmology do not sustain the truth of his second premise. It is more likely that the Big Bang was a transition event rather than an event of creation *ex nihilo*. A modern view of cosmology is presented by physicists Steinhardt and Turok in their book *Endless Universe*.

Huffling: "The evidence for the second premise [of Craig's kalam argument] is Big Bang cosmology. For example, the second law of

---

32. *God, Evil, and Morality*, 51.
33. *God, Evil, and Morality*, 51–52.
34. *God, Evil, and Morality*, 52.

thermodynamics states that usable energy is running out and if the universe were infinitely old it would have run out by now."[35]

The second law indirectly refers only to "usable energy," not all energy. In fact, the first law of thermodynamics says that all energy-matter is conserved and can be neither created nor destroyed. Therefore, it is likely that the universe is eternal and did not have a beginning from nothing.

Huffling: "There is no logical problem (per Aquinas) for such an infinite series; however, a *per se* ordered series of efficient causes, such as a hand moving a stick which moves a stone, could not be infinite."[36]

Neither Aquinas, Huffling, nor anyone else has proven that there could not be an infinite series of efficient causes. It appears that changes, especially in terms of causes and effects, are just an intrinsic and eternal feature of the universe. Just the way it is!

Huffling: "I have provided several philosophical arguments that God exists. These arguments must be analyzed and evaluated on their own terms. In other words, in order to reject them, one must refute them."[37]

I, and of course others, have analyzed, evaluated, rejected, and refuted all these tiresome and ancient philosophical arguments for God's existence which Huffling has presented. And yet Huffling has not refuted any of the arguments against God's existence which I have presented. To simplify our debate, I challenge him to focus on the argument about the Great Tsunami.

Huffling: "It will not do to claim that science has disproven God."[38]

It will do quite well to claim that reason, drawing on the disciplines of science, philosophy, and history, has disproven the existence of God. For the proof just look at the arguments I have presented.

---

35. *God, Evil, and Morality*, 52.
36. *God, Evil, and Morality*, 52–53.
37. *God, Evil, and Morality*, 53.
38. *God, Evil, and Morality*, 53.

8

God, Morality, and Aseity

J. Brian Huffling

It is interesting that Whittenberger thinks I am "begging the question" regarding God's existence when I have several arguments for such. The point he is responding to at the beginning of his last chapter is my statement that we need to *discover* what God is (or whether he is), rather than *stipulating* certain aspects about him. God's existence is a matter of investigation, not definition.

Whittenberger asserts that if his arguments about God's existence are sound then I am wasting my time with theistic proofs.[1] If his arguments are sound in demonstrating the non-existence of God, then I guess he would be right. However, *contra* his assertions, he has not demonstrated that God doesn't exist. He has a few variations of a single argument which attempts to demonstrate that if God exists then he wouldn't allow evil. Since evil exists, he says, God doesn't. As I have pointed out, to no avail, this type of thinking makes several assumptions, mainly (1) that God has obligations, (2) there is a logical contradiction with God and evil, and (3) God has no purpose with evil. I have argued (not asserting, *contra* Whittenberger) against all of these assumptions. Unfortunately, Whittenberger has refused to engage with my arguments.

My point with the "we already know God exists argument" is that there are good reasons for God, and evil does not negate those. When

---

1. *God, Evil, and Morality*, 55.

Whittenberger's arguments are deflated by rejecting his assumptions, the arguments fail.

I offered various cosmological arguments in my last chapter to which Whittenberger said I ignored his point about cosmology since he asserted that if the universe has always existed then it wouldn't need a cause.[2] However, in my last chapter I noted that Aquinas' arguments, particularly the second way, does not hinge on the temporal finitude of the universe. He actually didn't think reason alone could tell us that. The second way does not argue for a temporal beginning, but for a *cause of existence*. It wouldn't matter for this argument if the universe were infinitely old (if such an idea was even coherent).

Whittenberger's statement that even if the universe were contingent there'd be no reason to think its cause[3] would be "radically different" from the universe is interesting considering if God is the cause of energy-matter, then he couldn't be energy-matter. Thus, he would be immaterial. An immaterial being would by all counts (other than Whittenberger) be radically different from material being. Ockham's razor is not violated since it says *all things being equal*, causes shouldn't be multiplied. In this case, an immaterial cause creating matter is not equal to a material cause creating matter.

I would not call discussing the impossibility of an infinite regress a tangent in a debate about a necessary cause. It is also not clear why Whittenberger thinks Aristotle and Aquinas have not shown an impossibility of such causes when I explained their thinking in my last chapter. Simply put, if there is an infinity of intermediary causes there would be no first cause and thus no movement. This is the argument and Whittenberger has not attempted to refute it. Typically, in philosophy when an argument ends with an infinite regress it is a sign the argument is dead. Such has been the case with great thinkers, ancient and contemporary. Any argument that states the universe is infinite in the past has the problem of trying to traverse an infinite, which can't be done since quantitative or discrete infinites aren't real. Since moments in the past would be an actual infinite, such is impossible (this argument was made in my last chapter and not responded to).

I have stated that it is important for Whittenberger to explain where he is getting his standard definition, to which he responded by saying it comes from various sources including scripture (although scripture does not give philosophical notions of God), philosophers, etc. He then challenges me

---

2. *God, Evil, and Morality*, 55.
3. *God, Evil, and Morality*, 55.

"to ask a random sample of people shopping at a public mall what they think on the issue" of God being moral. He says he is "confident that most will see it as" he does.⁴

This is a very bizarre way to settle a philosophical point. I hardly think he would like this way of going about solving a complicated issue in psychology. Lay people are not versed in the discussions. Furthermore, I do not disagree that most people think God is a moral being. Such a challenge in this context strains credulity. Such also appears to commit the *argumentum ad populum* fallacy which points to the popular view as being true just because it's popular.

I have pointed out that thinkers like Augustine, Anselm, and Aquinas have been seen as "standard bearers" of orthodoxy. Whittenberger argues that they are too far in the past to be taken seriously.⁵ Apart from committing the *argumentum ab annis* fallacy, which says that truth is somehow based on time and changes with age, he betrays an ignorance of modern and contemporary theology, much of which is *based on* these thinkers. Even philosophical atheists take on such thinkers since they are still relevant to today's discussion. Aquinas in particular is tremendously important in contemporary work with some schools even having entire programs based around him. Protestants and Catholics praise him as one of the greatest thinkers in history and probably the greatest in Christian thought. To say I am cherry picking is to show his unfamiliarity with contemporary thought in this area, which is important given the topic of this debate.

While Whittenberger claims I have not explained how such thinkers reject the moral component of the standard definition,⁶ I have been arguing from the metaphysical position of Aquinas. I have alluded to this and have made inferences from his system while not citing Aquinas by name (explicitly), other than his arguments for God. Further, to be fair, there are Thomists who argue that Aquinas did maintain that there is an aspect in which God is moral since he is the cause of human morality, but such Thomists would deny that God is moral in the same way humans are, which is Whittenberger's and Shermer's position.

Whittenberger states he has "not yet challenged the existence of" Huffgod and also that he doubts he "will have time or space to address the

---

4. *God, Evil, and Morality*, 55.
5. *God, Evil, and Morality*, 56.
6. *God, Evil, and Morality*, 56.

existence of Huffgod."[7] This is an important point: I am arguing for what he calls "Huffgod" and he says he has not challenged the existence of my conception of God. Then by definition he has not challenged the conception of God I am *arguing* for. So, when he says he has demonstrated God doesn't exist, it's not the God I am arguing for. Thus, he has *not* demonstrated the God I am arguing for doesn't exist. Why does he keep arguing against a God that by his own admission *I am not arguing for*? Since this debate is with *me*, it should be about *my* arguments and conception of God, not what lay people think. The God I am arguing for is still on the table. I actually agree with Whittenberger that the God he is arguing about doesn't exist: a morally good God. I have argued that an infinite, transcendent, creator does not and cannot have moral obligations and thus is not moral. So, the God I am arguing for has not even been argued against, let alone disproven. This is because Whittenberger simply refuses to interact with my arguments.

He goes so far as to say "Huffling has presented no arguments" for God not being moral.[8] Such is demonstrably false. I did so in my response to Shermer's chapter and in my first response to Whittenberger (although less so since I laid out my case in responding to Shermer).[9] I presented a metaphysical position that says God is not the kind of being to be moral. In fact, in my written response to Shermer I made this *argument*:

1. If God is the creator of the universe, then he does not have properties of creation.
2. Morality is a property of creation.
3. Therefore, God does not have moral properties (i.e., he is not a moral being).

Interestingly, Whittenberger agrees that morality is a property of creation. He states, "By thinking rationally God would have created the moral standard before he created other persons." He names this view "correct universal ethics" or CUE. He states, "Henceforth, God would behave in accordance with CUE . . . ."[10] In chapter 5 he defines a moral being as "an intelligent agent who thinks about decisions within a moral framework and

---

7. *God, Evil, and Morality*, 56, 60.
8. *God, Evil, and Morality*, 58.
9. *God, Evil, and Morality*, 15–16, 28–32.
10. *God, Evil, and Morality*, 56.

attempts to comply with some standard of proper conduct."[11] Whittenberger claims that God "would thus have moral obligations to his creatures."[12]

There are a few problems with this. First, if being moral requires an intelligent being to make decisions in "a moral framework," and if CUE was created, and given Whittenberger's view of God being in time, then there was a time that God as an intelligent being existed without CUE. But that would remove a requirement for being moral. So at least at some "point" God would be amoral.

Second, if God created the laws of morality, then he transcends them. However, Whittenberger is maintaining that God acts in accordance with such laws. Whittenberger thus treats CUE as if it is transcendent over God. Such would be a contradiction.

Third, Whittenberger makes an explicit contradiction regarding this view of CUE and aseity. Aseity is the view that God depends on nothing—not just for existence, but for every aspect of his being, such as being good. Whittenberger has couched God's goodness in terms of moral goodness. Such moral goodness *depends* on his acting in accordance with CUE. However, if God is *a se*, then his goodness (whatever kind) *cannot depend* on anything. So, if Whittenberger's view of CUE is correct, then divine aseity is false. And if divine aseity is true, then Whittenberger's view of God and CUE must be false. These positions maintained by Whittenberger pose a contradiction. He does not see it this way. He declares, "God would be beholden to a moral standard *which he created*, and thus I am not denying aseity. There is no violation of the standard definition."[13]

Whittenberger simply does not understand the notion of divine aseity. As I have said, it is the notion that God depends on nothing for his being, goodness, etc. (It doesn't just mean God is uncaused, but that he *depends* on nothing else for anything.) Thus, divine aseity denies that God is beholden to *anything*. But Whittenberger maintains that God is beholden to something he *created*, namely CUE. In the literature on divine aseity, philosophers of religion debate how God relates to eternal and necessary truths, such as mathematical truths like 2+2=4 and statements like "murder is always wrong," or analytic truths like "all bachelors are unmarried men." Those in the Platonist tradition maintain that such truths are abstract objects (in the vein of Plato's Forms). God's relation to such eternal and

11. *God, Evil, and Morality*, 35.
12. *God, Evil, and Morality*, 37.
13. *God, Evil, and Morality*, 57. Emphasis in original.

necessary truths poses a problem to divine aseity since they are said to exist eternally and necessarily, like God. The question is, how can such things exist apart from God and God still be *a se* (self-existent and not dependent on anything)? Thus, philosophers of religion have very technical and important debates on this topic. This is because, by definition, created things are not necessary and eternal and thus depend on God for their "being." So, they pose no problem for divine aseity. Saying God is beholden to CUE to be morally good explicitly contradicts the doctrine of divine aseity.

My point is this: there is a contradiction with Whittenberger's notion of CUE and divine aseity which leads to a rejection of any classical notion of God, or as Whittenberger puts it, the standard definition. Whittenberger does not want to dispute what he sees as the standard definition; however, this is exactly what he is facing here. If he wants to maintain divine aseity, then he'll have to give up his notion of God's reliance on CUE. If he wants to hold on to CUE's relationship to God, he'll have to give up divine aseity. In other words, Whittenberger is going to have to argue for a position on God, not simply define him a certain way, since maintaining these two points leads to a contradiction.

Whittenberger and I both see morality as a property of creation; although, he holds that such a created property somehow affects God and I deny that. Very quickly I would like to point out two other ways in which CUE is in conflict with a classical view of God (the standard definition?). To say that created properties affect and change God denies divine simplicity and divine impassibility. The former says that God does not have any properties at all (in the Aristotelian sense) and the latter says that God is not affected by anything nor is he passive in any way. I do not want to turn this debate into one on God's attributes, but I do want to point out that denying three major classical doctrines on God demonstrates that Whittenberger is denying what he seems to be calling the standard definition. He certainly will find contemporary philosophers who reject simplicity and impassibility, but such are debates based on investigations on God and are not definitional issues. To take a stand on these positions, Whittenberger will have to argue and not stipulate.

Back to CUE. If Whittenberger is going to maintain that God is somehow related to CUE, he is going to need to show how such a relation is logically necessary or makes sense. His position is that it is *logically impossible* for God to exist given evil in the world. However, I think we have another contradiction here. For God to be logically required to abolish evil because of his relationship to CUE, his moral standing would have to be necessary and thus part of his nature. However, according to Whittenberger, morality is a created property. Since God didn't have to create, then he didn't have to create morality. Thus, God is not *necessarily* moral. Further, God was under no obligation to create CUE or to be voluntarily subordinate to it. Such obligation would have to logically pre-exist apart from CUE, but according to Whittenberger God is moral because of CUE. Thus, it seems God is not necessarily moral given that CUE is a contingent property of creation that God didn't have to make. Further, it has not been explained why God is necessarily related to CUE. In previous chapters Whittenberger has maintained that God is moral by virtue of being rational, but if he created CUE and was rational "before" creating it, then at some "time" God was rational and not moral. It seems Whittenberger wants to say that the very existence of CUE mandates God be beholden to it. But such would need an argument and demonstration. Again, such a *requirement* would transcend both God and CUE. But where would such a requirement come from? This would also pose problems for God's aseity. In short, God's relation to CUE, to say nothing of a *necessary* relation, is left unexplained and merely stipulated. It also won't do to simply point to the common view of God being moral. Nothing is or should be decided this way. We are dealing with technical issues of philosophy of religion that even philosophers in other fields are not generally familiar with, to say nothing of people at the mall.

In responding to my question of how do we know God is breaking some rule by allowing harm, Whittenberger says that he would be breaking MR#1, which says, "Person X should prevent harm to person Y, if he is able, unless allowing the harm is necessary for producing a greater gain and X also justifies this exception."[14] This rule is applicable to the various harm arguments Whittenberger provided. So, God would be in violation of MR#1 by allowing harm in a natural disaster. It is interesting Whittenberger allows for possible exceptions, such as there being "a greater gain" as long as this is justified. Given his position that it is logically impossible for a good God to exist, it would seem that Whittenberger would have to know *a priori* that there is no such greater gain to be had. But this seems wholly implausible, as theists have pointed out *ad nauseum*. There simply is no way for finite beings to know what an infinite being knows. Thus, there would at least seem to be a *logical possibility* that God knows of such gains that we don't know about which is why he allows some evil. But if this is the

---

14. *God, Evil, and Morality*, 58.

case, and it's hard to see how anyone could disagree with this, there would at least be a logical possibility that God could exist. At this point Whittenberger would have to demonstrate that there are no such gains, which by definition a finite being cannot do regarding an infinite one. At this point it seems like a stronger argument for Whittenberger to maintain is that God *probably* doesn't exist (a position more popular with philosophical atheists given the insurmountable difficulties in demonstrating there is no possibility for such reasons for evil). Such would seem especially the case since there would be no transcendent cause on God requiring him to behave in a certain way given Whittenberger thinks God created morality. Morality can't be simultaneously created by God and transcendent over God.

His reply is that there simply are no greater gains to be had given that God is an omni-God. However, if one is familiar with the literature on greater good arguments or best possible worlds, then it should be clear that such a position by Whittenberger is not logically airtight since he simply can't know what an infinite being knows. Such could account for greater gain. Or as I maintain, since God is not a human and not bound by human morality, maybe God simply decreed how things would be.

My position is "possible" but not "rational," according to Whittenberger.[15] But for something to be possible it would have to be rational. Here Whittenberger aligns himself with the notion that if God exists, he would be a person like humans. This view is known as theistic personalism and is condemned by classical theists. Such a view assumes a univocal view of "person." In other words, what is meant by "person" in reference to humans and God would be the same. Such could hardly be the case though given the differences between the two. My position is that God is analogous with respect to certain descriptions of humans, not univocal to them. For example, since humans and God do not have knowledge the same way, they have knowledge in an analogous way.

In connection with this, Whittenberger asks if I don't think God would use logic like us or make rational inferences like us from evidence.[16] No, I don't. I am not a theistic personalist. I am a classical theist who argues God is not in a temporal succession of moments and is impassible. Humans know because we infer from evidence over time in a passive way. Following Aquinas, I think God, as Pure Act, is not passive at all and is not temporal or changing. God knows all at once since he is the cause of finite being.

15. *God, Evil, and Morality*, 58.
16. *God, Evil, and Morality*, 60.

He doesn't learn. God learning would mean he is not infinite, perfect, or omniscient. Again, we have a contradiction with the classical (standard?) definition of God.

Here I am charged with special pleading and divine exceptionalism.[17] The former is ironic since I am arguing for my position and Whittenberger is admittedly stipulating it. The latter is simply false given the metaphysical differences between creator and created. Such is not exceptionalism but merely understanding the differences in kinds. Cats are not exceptions to dogs; cats just are not dogs. God is not an exception to human morality; God is simply not a human. God is not excepted from materiality; he just isn't material. Given Whittenberger's view that God *created* morality, it would seem that God is not subordinate to it since he would be transcendent over it.

At this point Whittenberger charges me with a contradiction. He quotes me as saying moral "principles are wholly obscure, unclear, and unexplained," while pointing out that in chapter 2, I said that "morality is something known rather intuitively."[18] Such would be a contradiction, except for the fact that in order for two propositions to contradict they would have to use the terms the same way with the same referent. In chapter 2, I was talking about our knowledge of everyday human morality. Regarding moral principles being unclear, I was asking about "these universal standards that God is beholden to" and from whence they come. I even noted that such principles don't exist, while I explicitly have maintained that human morality exists. Whittenberger simply didn't understand the contexts of these quotes and since they are different in meaning/referent they aren't contradictory.

I had previously said there are no scripture references that "say God will or must respond favorably to prayer."[19] Whittenberger provides several Bible verses that he takes to mean that God would.[20] Several of these have nothing to do with prayer for healing, etc., and are divorced form their context. James 5 is the most likely to be of such a candidate for what Whittenberger wants to say. In short, no one other than heretical groups like the Word of Faith Movement has taught that there is some guarantee of healing. A proper exposition of the passage is beyond the scope here. There

17. *God, Evil, and Morality*, 59.
18. *God, Evil, and Morality*, 59.
19. *God, Evil, and Morality*, 49.
20. *God, Evil, and Morality*, 61.

are various possible meanings of the passage. The word for "sick" can be physical illness or weakness. It is the same word Paul uses for himself in 2 Corinthians 12:9, where he says he has a "weakness" that God *refused* to remove for him. Contrary to those who think God is our genie, God is under no obligation to grant our every wish. As I said in my last chapter, nowhere does the Bible *guarantee* such a thing (that was my point, not that God will never, just that he is not under an obligation). In fact, it directly teaches against it, as Paul's case demonstrates. The Bible teaches that God's followers will suffer even as Jesus himself did. Christianity is not a religion that teaches we get our wish list from God. The references Whittenberger provided are simply taken out of context. I would point out too, that even if the Bible and Christianity were false, it would not prove God doesn't exist.

In wrapping up this chapter I would like to stress a point I have been making since the time of my oral debate with Shermer. In order to say that God can't exist alongside evil, we have to know what "God" and "evil" are. Whittenberger reduces evil to harm, but in so doing I think he fails to account for why harm is bad. Harm is bad because it prevents the attainment of good or happiness of the individual or thing. So, it seems there would have to be an account for *why* harm is bad that Whittenberger has not addressed.

But my main point is this: the only way we can say "God would or wouldn't do x" is to already know what God would be like. However, atheists like Shermer and Whittenberger (and even theists) usually do not start the investigation into God and evil like this. Usually one's notion of God precedes his view of the discussion. This is backwards. We have to know what God is like in order to say what we would or would not do.

9

Correct Universal Ethics and God's Transcendence

GARY J. WHITTENBERGER

As IN PREVIOUS CHAPTERS I will present key quotes of Huffling, this time from chapter 8, and will analyze and refute them.

Huffling: "God's existence is a matter of investigation, not definition."[1]

We use definitions during investigations, and so the existence of God is a matter of both investigation and definition.

Huffling: "However, *contra* his [Whittenberger's] assertions, he has not demonstrated that God doesn't exist."[2]

To the contrary, I have rationally demonstrated that God does not exist. I have provided four proofs and Huffling has found no fatal error in any of them.

Huffling: "As I have pointed out, to no avail, this type of thinking [by Whittenberger] makes several assumptions, mainly . . . (2) there is a logical contradiction with God and evil. . . . I have argued (not asserting, *contra* Whittenberger) against all of these assumptions. Unfortunately, Whittenberger has refused to engage with my arguments."[3]

Although Huffling keeps harping about "evil," my arguments do not address "evil," but instead address harm, suffering, and morality. Although

1. *God, Evil, and Morality*, 65.
2. *God, Evil, and Morality*, 65.
3. *God, Evil, and Morality*, 65.

he has objected to my arguments, he has failed to find any fatal error in any of them. My premises are correct, my logic is flawless, and so my conclusion is also correct—God does not exist. I have asked Huffling to focus on my argument regarding the Great Tsunami, but so far he has not done so.

Huffling: "My point with the 'we already know God exists argument' is that there are good reasons for God and evil does not negate those."[4]

There are no good reasons to conclude that God exists. Huffling has presented none. The best that can be said for the God hypothesis is that there is some evidence, e.g., the existence and the general orderliness of the universe itself, which is compatible with the existence of God, but this same evidence is compatible with the nonexistence of God. Thus, there is no unequivocal or conclusive evidence that God exists. Huffling's references to evil are irrelevant since my arguments focus on harm, suffering, and morality, and don't pertain to the obsolete concept of evil.

Huffling: "The second way [per Aquinas] does not argue for a temporal beginning, but for a *cause of existence*. It wouldn't matter for this argument if the universe were infinitely old (if such an idea was even coherent)."[5]

Causes occur in time, therefore if X causes the beginning of Y, then Y had a temporal beginning. If X caused the beginning of the universe, then the universe had a temporal beginning. Of course, the universe could be "infinitely old." Better to say "eternal." If anything could be eternal, then either God or the universe could be eternal. We know that the universe does exist, and many cosmologists now believe that the universe is eternal. We know that God does not exist, even though it had been hypothesized that he would be eternal if he did.

Huffling:

> Whittenberger's statement that even if the universe were contingent there'd be no reason to think its cause would be 'radically different' from the universe is interesting considering if God is the cause of energy-matter, then he couldn't be energy-matter. Thus, he would be immaterial. An immaterial being would by all counts (other than Whittenberger) be radically different from material being. Ockham's razor is not violated since it says *all things being equal*, causes shouldn't be multiplied. In this case, an immaterial cause creating matter is not equal to a material cause creating matter.[6]

4. *God, Evil, and Morality*, 65.
5. *God, Evil, and Morality*, 66. Emphasis in original.
6. *God, Evil, and Morality*, 66. Emphasis in original.

By definition, God would be composed of some unknown substance, which for now we can just call "spiritual substance," not energy-matter. Huffling has not shown that one form of energy-matter could not cause another form of energy-matter or that one part of the universe could not cause another part of it. He is violating Ockham's razor by multiplying types of substances or causes unnecessarily. Furthermore, there is no good evidence that spiritual substance even exists.

Huffling: "Simply put, if there is an infinity of intermediary causes there would be no first cause and thus no movement."[7]

This is muddled thinking. Why should anyone conclude that there is "an infinity of intermediary causes"? Intermediary between what and what? There are movements and there are sequences of cause and effect. It is a reasonable inference that movements, causes, and effects continue into the infinite past and into the infinite future. If this inference is correct, then there would be no first cause and no last cause.

Huffling: "Any argument that states the universe is infinite in the past has the problem of trying to traverse an infinite, which can't be done since-quantitative or descrete infinites aren't real."[8]

This makes no sense. Huffling is imagining a problem, i.e., "traversing an infinite," where there is none. Here is a model which actually works: Between any two points in time the number of events between them is finite, but events continue endlessly into the past and the future. The set of all events is infinite. Where's the problem?

Huffling: "He [Whittenberger] then challenges me 'to ask a random sample of people shopping at a public mall what they think on the issue' of God being moral. He says he is 'confident that most will see it as' he does.

This is a very bizarre way to settle a philosophical point."[9]

The concept of God was invented thousands of years ago, and over the millennia the concept has been tweaked and reshaped. Now, there is a common understanding of it among the nearly eight billion people on earth. How could we assess that common understanding? One way is by a broad scientific survey. My suggestion of an informal survey of people in a mall is just an informal approximation to that. The definition of "God" is as much an empirical point as it is a philosophical one.

---

7. *God, Evil, and Morality*, 66.
8. *God, Evil, and Morality*, 66.
9. *God, Evil, and Morality*, 66–77.

Huffling: "Furthermore, I do not disagree that most people think God is a moral being. Such a challenge in this context strains credulity. Such also appears to commit the *argumentum ad populum* fallacy which points to the popular view as being true just because it's popular."[10]

I am pleased that Huffling agrees that most people define or understand God as a moral being. Indeed, it would strain credulity if Huffling disagreed. If I were claiming that God exists because most people believe he exists, then I would be committing the "*argumentum ad populum* fallacy." But I am claiming no such thing! In fact, I am claiming that God does not exist because it is the conclusion to four sound arguments. I have challenged Huffling to focus on one of those arguments, i.e., the Great Tsunami argument, and so far he has just evaded the challenge.

Huffling: "I have pointed out that thinkers like Augustine, Anselm, and Aquinas have been seen as 'standard bearers' of orthodoxy. Whittenberger argues that they are too far in the past to be taken seriously."[11]

I have taken seriously and refuted every point that Huffling has made on behalf of Augustine, Anselm, and Aquinas in this discussion. These authors are not mistaken because they are ancient. They are mistaken because they have violated the methods and principles of reason. Because they are ancient, they did not have the advantages of advances in reason that have occurred since they lived. For scientists, compare Ptolemy from the past to Paul Steinhardt today. For philosophers, compare Augustine from the past to Sam Harris today. The current experts are more likely to be correct than the ancient ones. Besides, were Augustine, Anselm, and Aquinas philosophers or just theologians? Probably the latter.

Huffling: "While Whittenberger claims I have not explained how such thinkers reject the moral component of the standard definition, I have been arguing from the metaphysical position of Aquinas."[12]

Huffling is just beating around the bush. Did Aquinas think that God was a moral being or not? Where are the quotes from this author relevant to this topic?

Huffling: "I am arguing for what he [Whittenberger] calls 'Huffgod' and he says he has not challenged the existence of my conception of God.

---

10. *God, Evil, and Morality*, 67.
11. *God, Evil, and Morality*, 67.
12. *God, Evil, and Morality*, 67.

Then by definition he has not challenged the conception of God I am *arguing for.*"[13]

If Huffling wants to defend the existence of some god other than God, e.g., Huffgod, that's just fine, but that's a topic for another debate. By the standard definition, God is a moral being, I have proven by four sound arguments that God does not exist, and neither Huffling nor anyone else has yet found a fatal flaw in these arguments. Now would be a good time for Huffling to just concede the truth of the conclusion—God does not exist!

Huffling: "So, when he says he has demonstrated God doesn't exist, it's not the God I am arguing for."[14]

Here Huffling makes a common error—he confuses a category with a particular within the category. The category is "gods." But "God" is only one particular among many within the category. "Huffgod" is another particular in the category. These particulars differ in at least one important respect. God is a moral being, but Huffgod is an amoral being. I will correct Huffling's statement to this: "So, when Whittenberger says he has demonstrated God doesn't exist, it's not the particular god I am arguing for." Huffling wants to argue for the existence of Huffgod, but I am arguing against the existence of God.

Huffling: "I actually agree with Whittenberger that the God he is arguing about doesn't exist: a morally good God."[15]

Here Huffling continues to repeat his mistake of confusing the concepts 'god' and 'God.' Nevertheless, he has agreed with me that the god which I have clearly defined and who is endorsed by most people in the world, i.e., God, doesn't exist. Game over! Huffling belongs to a small minority of persons who believe in the existence of an amoral god, i.e., Huffgod, but belief in this god is not rationally warranted.

Huffling: "I presented a metaphysical position that says God is not the kind of being to be moral. In fact, in my written response to Shermer I made this argument:

1. If God is the creator of the universe, then he does not have properties of creation.

2. Morality is a property of creation.

---

13. *God, Evil, and Morality*, 68.
14. *God, Evil, and Morality*, 68.
15. *God, Evil, and Morality*, 68.

3. Therefore, God does not have moral properties (i.e., he is not a moral being).[16]

I did not recall this poorly stated argument, but the first two premises are false and so the argument fails. According to the standard definition God is a hypothetical being who is not only the creator but is also perfectly moral. If God were the creator of the universe, then he would have a creative property, and he could create anything he wanted because he would be omnipotent. It is possible that God could have some of the properties of the universe, e.g., orderliness, which he created. Finally, morality would not be a "property" of creation; it would be a product of a creative act of God.

Huffling: "Whittenberger agrees that morality is a property of creation."[17]

This is incorrect. I believe morality would be a product of a creative act of God, if he existed. If God did exist, he would have created the universe, persons in it, and morality to govern behavior. He might have done this in a sequence of acts, as Genesis speculates, or he might have done it in one act. It doesn't matter with respect to my arguments.

Huffling: ". . . then there was a time that God as an intelligent being existed without CUE. But that would remove a requirement for being moral. So at least at some 'point' [in time] God would be amoral."[18]

I think Huffling and I agree on this point. God would have been amoral before he created other persons, but perfectly moral after he created them. In a sense God added a property to himself, and he became perfectly moral.

Huffling: ". . . if God created the laws of morality, then he transcends them. However, Whittenberger is maintaining that God acts in accordance with such laws. Whittenberger thus treats CUE as if it is transcendent over God. Such would be a contradiction."[19]

Here Huffling misunderstands the concept of transcendence. God would be transcendent over CUE since he created it. But after he created CUE, he decided to conform to it. CUE specifies how persons should and should not behave with respect to each other. God would conform to his own commands. There is no contradiction.

16. *God, Evil, and Morality*, 68.
17. *God, Evil, and Morality*, 68.
18. *God, Evil, and Morality*, 69.
19. *God, Evil, and Morality*, 69.

Huffling:

> Whittenberger makes an explicit contradiction regarding this view of CUE and aseity. Aseity is the view that God depends on nothing—not just for existence, but for every aspect of his being, such as being good. Whittenberger has couched God's goodness in terms of moral goodness. Such moral goodness *depends* on his acting in accordance with CUE. However, if God is *a se*, then his goodness (whatever kind) *cannot depend* on anything. So, if Whittenberger's view of CUE is correct, then divine aseity is false. And if divine aseity is true, then Whittenberger's view of God and CUE must be false. These positions maintained by Whittenberger pose a contradiction.[20]

Theologians have called God "perfectly good" or "perfectly loving" or "omnibenevolent." But what do these concepts mean with respect to other persons? They mean that God would treat other persons properly, i.e., he would be perfectly moral! I have just presented a reasonable account of how God might have become perfectly moral, if he existed. God's aseity would not be changed by having become perfectly moral. He would not be dependent on anything, but he would conform to rules of his own creation. God would not be a hypocrite.

Huffling: "Whittenberger simply does not understand the notion of divine aseity. . . . Thus, divine aseity denies that God is beholden to *anything*."[21]

I disagree that I don't understand the concept. I have simply used the definition of "aseity" provided by the *Pocket Dictionary of Theological Terms*, cited in chapter 7. I think Huffling may be misunderstanding the concept. To be beholden to something is not necessarily to be dependent on it. God would be beholden to CUE after he created it, but he would not be dependent on it. As long as there are other persons God would conform to CUE 100 percent of the time. This means that he would be perfectly moral. Perhaps we can think of God as having primary and secondary properties. A primary property might be "omni-creative," while a secondary property might be "being the creator and ruler of the universe." Similarly, another primary property might be "omni-rational," while a secondary property might be "perfectly moral." As a result of being omni-rational and omni-creative and intending to create other persons, God would necessarily

20. *God, Evil, and Morality*, 69. Emphasis in original.
21. *God, Evil, and Morality*, 69. Emphasis in original.

invent CUE—a set of moral rules which all persons should follow. Secondary properties would be a result of primary properties.

Huffling: "God's relation to such eternal and necessary truths [Plato's Forms] poses a problem to divine aseity since they are said to exist eternally and necessarily, like God. The question is, how can such things exist apart from God and God still be *a se* (self-existent and not dependent on anything)?"[22]

I have never endorsed Plato's Forms. Furthermore, moral propositions are neither true nor false. They are prescriptive, not descriptive. I have never claimed that CUE existed "eternally and necessarily." I claimed that if God did exist, he created CUE! God can still be "*a se*" even though he creates stuff, like a universe, other persons, and CUE. God's moral perfection would be a consequence of, not a contradiction to, God's aseity.

Huffling: "If he wants to maintain divine aseity, then he'll have to give up his notion of God's reliance on CUE. If he wants to hold on to CUE's relationship to God, he'll have to give up divine aseity. In other words, Whittenberger is going to have to argue for a position on God, not simply define him a certain way since maintaining these two points leads to a contradiction."[23]

This analysis is flawed, and I have already shown why. Aseity would be a primary property of God, whereas "perfectly moral" would be a secondary property. God would have added a property to himself. This is a perfectly rational explanation. There is no contradiction.

Huffling: "To say that created properties affect and change God denies divine simplicity and divine impassibility. The former says that God does not have any properties at all (in the Aristotelian sense) and the latter says that God is not affected by anything nor is he passive in any way."[24]

The universe, other persons, and CUE would not be "created properties," if God did exist. They would be *products* of his creation! If God did exist, he would have added the properties of "creator of the universe" and "perfectly moral" to himself. My understanding of the idea of divine simplicity is that God would not have internal parts; he would not be like a machine. I don't take a position on this hypothesis, but it is not included in the standard definition. According to that definition, God has properties, and I have listed the main ones. Huffling's definition of "impassibility" is

22. *God, Evil, and Morality*, 69–70.
23. *God, Evil, and Morality*, 70.
24. *God, Evil, and Morality*, 70.

vague, but God would be affected by some things. For example, God would be pleased when the persons he created conformed to CUE and displeased when they did not. In addition, he would react to some problems on the earth by performing miracles. Most persons today who believe in God think that he has performed some miracles.

Huffling: "If Whittenberger is going to maintain that God is somehow related to CUE, he is going to need to show how such a relation is logically necessary or makes sense. His position is that it is *logically impossible* for God to exist given evil in the world."[25]

I have already shown what God's relationship to CUE would be. He would have decided to create other persons, he rationally knew that persons should interact with each other in certain ways and not in other ways, and so he created CUE, which he decided to conform to. He would not be a hypocrite; he would comply with the moral rules which he created. I have discarded the obsolete concept of "evil" in my account. I don't know why Huffling keeps bringing it up. It's a red herring.

Huffling: "Since God didn't have to create, then he didn't have to create morality. Thus, God is not *necessarily* moral. Further, God was under no obligation to create CUE or to be voluntarily subordinate to it."[26]

If God did exist, he would be free to do whatever he wanted, but he would have wanted to create and indeed he would have created. Huffling and others hypothesize that he created a universe, human persons, and possibly other persons like angels or aliens. Being maximally rational, he would have created or invented rules to govern the interactions of persons. I have called this set of rules "correct universal ethics." God was not meeting an obligation in creating CUE, but he was behaving according to his rational nature in doing so. Not interested in carving out an exception for himself, not wanting to be a hypocrite, and being perfectly rational, God voluntarily chose to conform to CUE. This is a perfectly reasonable explanation, if God were to exist. On the other hand, Huffling's god, i.e., Huffgod, supposedly created morality for others, but not for himself. On this point Huffling is engaged in special pleading.

Huffling: "In previous chapters Whittenberger has maintained that God is moral by virtue of being rational, but if he created CUE and was

---

25. *God, Evil, and Morality*, 70. Emphasis in original.
26. *God, Evil, and Morality*, 71. Emphasis in original.

rational 'before' creating it, then at some 'time' God was rational and not moral."[27]

Yes, I mostly agree with this. God would have become perfectly moral by virtue of being maximally creative, all-powerful, and perfectly rational. His perfectly moral nature would have been derived from other more basic properties. If only one person existed, i.e., God, then morality would have no value. If God created other persons, then God created rational rules for the interaction of all persons. Being a rational fellow, God would not exempt himself.

Huffling: "Given his position that it is logically impossible for a good God to exist, it would seem that Whittenberger would have to know *a priori* that there is no such greater gain to be had. But this seems wholly implausible as theists have pointed out *ad nauseum*."[28]

It is not logically impossible for a good God to exist! Once again, Huffling is trying to sneak in concepts or terms which I have not used or have discarded. Before it was "evil," and in this chapter it is "good." These are irrelevant to my argument. Also here, when he talks about a "greater gain to be had," he leaves out an essential part of MR#1: ". . . unless allowing the harm is necessary for producing a greater gain." Because God would be all-powerful there would no necessity! For God, the harm would not be necessary for producing a greater gain since he could easily produce whatever gain was to be had without allowing the harm. Theists have ignored this point *ad nauseum*.

Huffling: "There simply is no way for finite beings to know what an infinite being knows. Thus, there would at least seem to be *a logical possibility* that God knows of such gains that we don't know about, which is why he allows some evil. At this point Whittenberger would have to demonstrate that there are no such gains, which by definition a finite being cannot do regarding an infinite one."[29]

We measly human beings can and do know that it wouldn't be necessary for the hypothetical God to allow the Great Tsunami in order to enable gains to come from it. Because God would be all-powerful, he would not be bound by the "necessities" by which we are bound. It is not incumbent on me to demonstrate that there are no gains that could be had, but it is incumbent on Huffling to demonstrate that there are gains because of which

---

27. *God, Evil, and Morality*, 71.
28. *God, Evil, and Morality*, 71.
29. *God, Evil, and Morality*, 71–72. Emphasis in original.

God *must* allow the harm and suffering coming from the Great Tsunami. But my opponent cannot do this because by definition God is all-powerful and need not allow the harms from the Tsunami. In addition, Huffling continues to make the same errors as before—using "infinite" and "finite" without referring to specific traits and to use the obsolete and unnecessary concept of "evil."

Huffling has also ignored another essential part of MR#1: ". . . and X also justifies this exception."[30] For example, if God were to allow the Great Tsunami, causing immense harm to human persons, then he would justify to the world why he allowed it. He would present his reasons to the victims, their families and friends, and all of humanity. A moral person doesn't allow harm, when he could stop it, and then not tell others why.

Huffling: "Morality can't be simultaneously created by God and transcendent over God."[31]

As I mentioned before, God would be transcendent over anything he creates, he would have created the universe, other persons, and CUE, and thus he would be transcendent over all of these. However, because of his perfect rationality he would have chosen to conform to CUE 100 percent of the time, which made himself "perfectly moral."

Huffling: ". . . it should be clear that such a position by Whittenberger is not logically airtight since he simply can't know what an infinite being knows."[32]

Fortunately, Huffling, other persons, and I can and do know that God himself would know that allowing the harm of the Tsunami would be completely unnecessary for him. He could produce any possible gains with no harm or less harm. After all, he would be all-knowing and all-powerful. And so, my position is logically airtight.

Huffling: "Whittenberger aligns himself with the notion that if God exists, he would be a person like humans. This view is known as theistic personalism and is condemned by classical theists."[33]

I don't know why Huffling keeps harping on this; we have already covered it. I have made it clear that if God did exist, he would be both similar to and different from human persons, and I have outlined how this would be. According to the standard definition, God would not be a force, a law, an

---

30. *God, Evil, and Morality*, 58.
31. *God, Evil, and Morality*, 72.
32. *God, Evil, and Morality*, 72.
33. *God, Evil, and Morality*, 72.

animal, or a machine. He would be a person or intelligent agent! Huffling's preferred god, i.e., Huffgod, would be an amoral person, but God would be a perfectly moral person.

Huffling: "Following Aquinas, I think God, as Pure Act, is not passive at all and is not temporal or changing."[34]

Although God would act, he would not be "Pure Act." That is theological mumbo-jumbo, and Aquinas was well known for that kind of sophistry. Huffling is contradicting himself by implying that God would be "not passive" and passive ("not changing") at the same time.

Huffling: "God knows all at once since he is the cause of finite being. He doesn't learn. God learning would mean he is not infinite, perfect, or omniscient."[35]

God could be the cause of finite beings without knowing everything all at once, so Huffling has produced a *non sequitur* here. Huffling continues to refer to God as "infinite" and "perfect," but fails to use these concepts to refer to traits. And so, it is fair to ask, "Would God be infinitely, or perfectly, malevolent?" It is a live controversy among philosophers whether God would have or could have foreknowledge of the free acts of human persons. If he would not or could not have this kind of knowledge, then he could indeed learn that such acts occurred and their consequences. At any rate, God would know about the harms to be caused by the Great Tsunami and would prevent those harms or perhaps the entire Tsunami because he would be both all-powerful and perfectly moral, as I have explained before.

Huffling: "Here I am charged with special pleading and divine exceptionalism. The former is ironic since I am arguing for my position and Whittenberger is admittedly stipulating it."[36]

To be clear I am using the standard definition of God which includes "perfectly moral" as a trait or property. So, in a sense I am stipulating what most human persons throughout history have thought and what most now continue to think about God. And then I have argued that this god does not exist by using evidence and logic. Huffling takes a slightly different approach. He looks at the world and argues that if any creator god did exist, surely it must be amoral. That's a possibility, but reality could be otherwise. This creating god might be extremely malevolent or sadistic or might be partly moral and partly immoral. Furthermore, Huffling provides very

---

34. *God, Evil, and Morality*, 72.
35. *God, Evil, and Morality*, 72–73.
36. *God, Evil, and Morality*, 73.

weak arguments that a creator god exists. So, we both make arguments, but take different approaches. When all is said and done, Huffgod very probably does not exist and God definitely does not exist.

Huffling: "The latter [the claim that Huffling embraces the doctrine of divine exceptionality] is simply false given the metaphysical differences between creator and created. Such is not exceptionalism but merely understanding the differences in kinds. Cats are not exceptions to dogs; cats just are not dogs. God is not an exception to human morality; God is simply not a human."[37]

CUE is for all persons, not just human persons! Apparently Huffling fails to accept what most believers already accept—that God would be a person. And if he would be a person, then he is not to be exempted from CUE through special pleading because he happens to be super creative and creator of a universe. God would not be exempted from CUE, like President Trump is not exempted from norms, laws, and the constitution. Huffling may see the differences between divine and human agents, but he doesn't appreciate the similarities. To be a person is to be a moral agent. Cats are not dogs, but both are mammals. The gods are not humans, but both are persons. God would be a divine person, while we intelligent residents of the earth are human persons. To assert that God would not be a human is a straw man.

Huffling: "Contrary to those who think God is our genie, God is under no obligation to grant our every wish. As I said in my last chapter, nowhere does the Bible *guarantee* such a thing (that was my point, not that God will never, just that he is not under an obligation)."[38]

Here Huffling has forgotten or failed to review what he actually claimed! In chapter 6 Huffling said "Nowhere [in the Bible] does it say that God will or must respond favorably to prayer."[39] That may not be what Huffling intended to claim, but there it is, and the claim is just plain false! I presented six verses which refuted his claim. Of course I took the verses out of context; that's what people do when they extract quotations. But a consideration of the broader context of those verses does not negate my refutation. Rather, the broader context reinforces it! If God did exist, he would not break his promises or predictions.

---

37. *God, Evil, and Morality*, 73.
38. *God, Evil, and Morality*, 74. Emphasis in original.
39. *God, Evil, and Morality*, 49.

Huffling: "In order to say that God can't exist alongside evil, we have to know what 'God' and 'evil' are. Whittenberger reduces evil to harm, but in so doing I think he fails to account for why harm is bad. Harm is bad because it prevents the attainment of good or happiness of the individual or thing."[40]

Huffling continues to talk about evil, when my arguments do not mention it. If he wants to refute one argument in particular, then he will need to address the harm produced by the Great Tsunami, and he hasn't done this. Why is harm bad? That seems like a very odd question. One reasonable answer is that harm is just intrinsically bad. Another reasonable answer is that harm is bad because it interferes with the inherent objectives of persons, whereas help is good because it facilitates the inherent objectives of persons. Perhaps harm and help are simply deviations from neutral, like shifting a car into forward or reverse from the neutral or park position.

Huffling: "But my main point is this: the only way we can say 'God would or wouldn't do x' is to already know what God would be like."[41]

If this is Huffling's main point, then it is simply mistaken. We've already been over this issue more than once. We can reasonably say what God would or wouldn't do by making rational predictions or derivations from his assumed nature which is presented in the standard definition. These predictions are contradicted by the evidence of the world. God is not like a woodpecker which we can describe first-hand. God is a hypothetical thing that, if it existed, would manifest itself in the universe in some ways and not others. And so, if God did exist, some things would not even exist in our world. One such thing is the Great Tsunami. Nevertheless, it happened. It is clear what this means—God does not exist!

---

40. *God, Evil, and Morality*, 74.
41. *God, Evil, and Morality*, 74.

10

God, Moral Propositions, and Truth

J. BRIAN HUFFLING

BEFORE I RESPOND TO Whittenberger's individual points, I'd like to make some general responses to themes that run throughout his last chapter and previous chapters.

The entirety of this debate has centered around the possibility of God existing in the face of evil, suffering, or harm. Shermer laid out, as did I, the standard logical form of the problem of evil. My central point both with Shermer and Whittenberger is to maintain that there is no logical problem if we remove a necessary assumption to that problem. Even J. L. Mackie, a central defender of the logical argument, maintained that there is a logical problem only given such assumptions. He admits that if those are taken away, such as the notion that God is all-good, then the problem goes away. I have attempted to do just that: remove a central assumption to the argument by demonstrating that God is not good in the sense the argument requires. I am not the first person to do this.

However, rather than dealing with my central point, Whittenberger has maintained that he wants to abide by a mere definition of God that he argues most people abide by. I have assented that most people today do abide by the standard definition in the way he has described it, viz., that God is morally perfect. I have also maintained that most theologians and philosophers throughout church history have maintained that God is good but not necessarily *morally* good in the way that humans are, and certainly not by having obligations. Typically, in debates the two opposing sides focus on the central tenet(s) of the debate. However, Whittenberger has refused to do this and instead has rested his entire position on an admitted stipulated definition of God. This has been disappointing. He has said multiple times that he is not debating my view of God, which is hard to understand since the debate is *with me*. During a formal debate, which this is not exactly, if a debater refuses to interact and deal with a major aspect of his opponent, he pretty much loses the debate by default. It is hard to understand why he doesn't want to *argue* for his position but rather *stipulate* his position, especially when that is the entire question of the debate.

This is simply not how philosophy is done. Philosophers, simply as a matter of fact, do not merely stipulate their position. Rather, they argue for it. While Whittenberger states that "the existence of God is a matter of both investigation and definition," this is simply false. There is nothing that is proved to exist or not simply by its definition (*pace* Anselm).

Whittenberger says that I have not found a "fatal error in any of" his four arguments against God;[1] however, such is demonstrably false. First, I have stated that they are really four variations of just *one* argument. Second, I have called the first premise into question by saying it assumes that God is a moral being with obligations. I have argued that such is simply not the case. God as a transcendent being is not a moral being and has no moral obligations. If I am right, the first premise is false, rendering the argument unsound. I have said this several times, so the fact that Whittenberger says I haven't addressed his argument seems to indicate he either doesn't realize that or is ignoring it. His response to my arguments that God is not moral is simply to reject what I am saying, say his position is true by definition, and then declare his arguments victorious, all the while saying I have not attempted to refute his arguments. If arguing against the first premise of his argument(s) doesn't count as interacting with or refuting his arguments, then nothing will.

Whittenberger has argued that he does not want this discussion to be couched in terms of "evil" but of harm or suffering.[2] For the following reasons I have maintained my use of the term "evil." First, this project started out as an oral debate between me and Michael Shermer. It then progressed to a print dialogue in *Skeptic* between us and then me and Whittenberger. Second, it is the normal term used by both atheists and theists in this debate. Third, the distinction Whittenberger makes between "evil," "harm,"

---

1. *God, Evil, and Morality*, 75.
2. *God, Evil, and Morality*, 75.

and "suffering" seems to be a distinction without a difference. Atheists often use the same examples Whittenberger does and they call them "evil." Fourth, there is an aspect lost in the discussion when the notion of evil is not used. When everything bad that happens is reduced to harm and suffering, the entire discussion is reduced to materialism. Whittenberger rejects the notion of evil as merely a religious idea,[3] but this is false since atheists use the term as well as an argument *against* religion. The notion of evil is not a material notion like harm and suffering. It is a description of *behavior* or *events*. But if we merely talk about harm and suffering, we cannot describe people like Hitler very well. By any standard Hitler is rightly thought of as evil. If Whittenberger wants to say that Hitler was a bad person or the like, I would argue such a distinction has no difference. Also, Whittenberger seems to lose his argument if he jettisons the moral notion of evil—there's no necessarily *moral* sense to harm and suffering in terms of a wrong being done like we have with evil. A tsunami causes harm, but Whittenberger is charging God with *evil* in letting it happen. He says God has *moral* obligations, like humans. What is he charging God with if the notion of evil is off the table? What is the opposite of God being morally perfect? Whittenberger himself says that it is possible for God to be malevolent, which to me sounds like evil. Let me now respond to some of the more specific issues he raises.

In responding to Aquinas' second way Whittenberger says, "Causes occur in time, therefore if X causes the beginning of Y, then Y had a temporal beginning."[4] This is the case with natural causes but says nothing about a supernatural cause. Since Whittenberger is adamant about maintaining a standard definition, such a definition would need to include God being eternal. Whittenberger further notes that "the universe could be 'infinitely old.'"[5] Whittenberger seems to miss Aquinas' point since I explicitly stated that Aquinas' second way does not depend on the temporal finitude of the universe. Rather, it argues for the impossibility of an infinite regress of efficient causes, in time or not.

He next argues that God must be composed of some sort of spiritual substance and that I have "not shown that one form of energy-matter could not cause another form of energy-matter or that one part of the universe

---

3. *God, Evil, and Morality*, 59.
4. *God, Evil, and Morality*, 76.
5. *God, Evil, and Morality*, 76.

could not cause another part of it."[6] That's not the issue. The point I was making is that if God is *immaterial* then he is different from material beings. This gets at the heart of my position that God being unlike humans is not held to human standards. I have not violated Ockham's razor as he alleges since I have not multiplied causes needlessly. I am arguing for a transcendent cause of the universe and ironically so did Ockham (he was a theist). Is Whittenberger going to accuse Ockham of violating Ockham's razor?

Returning to the cosmological argument, Whittenberger says that my assertion (*a la* Aquinas) that if there were an infinite number of intermediary causes there would be no first cause is "muddled thinking."[7] Such is of course, merely rhetorical. He continues, "Why should anyone conclude that there is 'an infinity of intermediary causes'? Intermediary between what and what? There are movements and there are sequences of cause and effect. It is a reasonable inference that movements, causes, and effects continue into the infinite past and into the infinite future. If this inference is correct, then there would be no first cause and no last cause."[8] If there would be an infinite number of causes in the past, then there would by definition be no first cause but an infinite number of intermediary ones (Aquinas' point, actually). In the context of the argument, they would be intermediary between the first cause and the effect. However, if there is no first cause, as Whittenberger admits there wouldn't be, there would be no effects either. The argument is meant to show that since there are effects, there must be a first cause.

A problem that Aquinas and others have is that of an infinite regress. Another problem is actually traversing an infinite, which the Muslim philosophers pointed out. If time goes backwards infinitely and now is the latest moment in a series of infinite moments, then we would not have arrived at this moment since an actual infinity can't be traversed. Whittenberger states, "This makes no sense. Huffling is imagining a problem, i.e., 'traversing an infinite,' where there is none."[9] Such is false. I am just one of many philosophers throughout history who sees this problem. Saying it "makes no sense" is not a response, but only demonstrates that Whittenberger doesn't understand the issue.

6. *God, Evil, and Morality*, 77.
7. *God, Evil, and Morality*, 77.
8. *God, Evil, and Morality*, 77.
9. *God, Evil, and Morality*, 77.

He says he has "taken seriously and refuted every point which Huffling has made on behalf of . . . Aquinas."[10] I think it is demonstrably false that he has refuted every point of, say, Aquinas. I would argue he hasn't addressed or even understood Aquinas. Further, he claims such thinkers aren't wrong because they are old (which he later contradicts by saying the later thinkers have more advanced reasoning), but "because they have violated the methods and principles of reason."[11] This statement is wholly obscure. What principle of logic have they violated? Such general critiques are frowned upon in philosophy and comes across as merely rhetorical. Whittenberger asks, "Besides, were Augustine, Anselm, and Aquinas philosophers or just theologians? Probably the latter."[12] It is not debated among philosophers whether they were philosophers as well as theologians. It is curious what Whittenberger's point is here. It seems he is disparaging them for being "just theologians." But being theologians is still relevant to this discussion. It is not clear why a psychologist is castigating theologians for not being philosophers when Whittenberger himself is not a trained philosopher.

I am accused of "beating around the bush" concerning my argument from such thinkers as Aquinas that God is not moral.[13] As I have said, I am arguing for Aquinas' metaphysical position that God is radically different from creation. While Aquinas nowhere explicitly states "God is not moral," what he thinks human morality is, in following Aristotle, *cannot* be attributed to God, as it would require Aquinas to contradict his earlier positions such as simplicity and everything he thinks God is. God was not thought of as a moral being like humans in the Middle Ages, so it would not have been important for Aquinas to refute a position that didn't really exist.

While I have addressed his next objection already, I think it's worth noting again. He writes, "If Huffling wants to defend the existence of some god other than God, e.g., Huffgod, that's just fine, but that's a topic for another debate."[14] I simply can't get my head around this. *This is the debate we are having*. It was the debate that he responded to in *Skeptic* when I was debating Shermer. It is simply inexplicable why Whittenberger ignores my *main point* that attacks the first premises of his arguments by removing a necessary assumption, and then says it really isn't germane to this

10. *God, Evil, and Morality*, 78.
11. *God, Evil, and Morality*, 78.
12. *God, Evil, and Morality*, 78.
13. *God, Evil, and Morality*, 78.
14. *God, Evil, and Morality*, 79.

discussion. *This is the heart of the discussion.* I don't care about a "standard definition" that has still never been referenced. I care about debunking the false notion that God is a moral being and is required to follow human moral codes.

When I pointed out that the God he says doesn't exist is not the God I'm arguing for, he responded, "Here Huffling makes a common error—he confuses a category with a particular within the category. The category is 'gods.' But 'God' is only one particular among many within the category. 'Huffgod' is another particular in the category."[15] I'm not sure what his point is here. He says he "will correct [my] statement to this: 'So, when Whittenberger says he has demonstrated God doesn't exist, it's not the particular god I am arguing for.' Huffling wants to argue for the existence of Huffgod, but I am arguing against the existence of God."[16] I really don't see a relevant difference in our two statements except to again point out Whittenberger refuses to interact with my main position.

When I state my agreement with Whittenberger that the morally good God he is referring to doesn't exist, he thinks it is "Game over!"[17] How could this be if we are by definition not debating the same issue? He is arguing that X doesn't exist and I am arguing Y exists. Logically, agreeing that X doesn't exist has nothing to say about Y. Since Whittenberger is admittedly not debating my God, there is no game to be over. I have never argued in this debate that a morally good God exists but have consistently maintained no such God exists, which solves the alleged problem of evil (as it is universally called). He asserts that belief in Huffgod "is not rationally warranted."[18] However, he has not interacted with, let alone refuted, my view of God.

At this point Whittenberger addresses my argument, which is:

1. If God is the creator of the universe, then he does not have properties of creation.

2. Morality is a property of creation.

3. Therefore, God does not have moral properties (i.e., he is not a moral being).

---

15. *God, Evil, and Morality*, 79.
16. *God, Evil, and Morality*, 79.
17. *God, Evil, and Morality*, 79.
18. *God, Evil, and Morality*, 79.

He responds: "I did not recall this poorly stated argument, but the first two premises are false and so the argument fails. According to the standard definition God is a hypothetical being who is not only the creator but is also perfectly moral. If God were the creator of the universe, then he would have a creative property, and he could create anything he wanted because he would be omnipotent. It is possible that God could have some of the properties of the universe, e.g., orderliness, which he created."[19] It is not clear what it even means for an argument to be "poorly stated." Deductive arguments like this are either valid or invalid and either sound or unsound. Premises can be true or false and terms can be clear or unclear. Inductive arguments can be cogent or not. He has not addressed my argument; he has ignored it.

The standard definition, whatever that is, is completely irrelevant to my argument. Philosophers are allowed and expected to make arguments, even if they do go against typical views. The argument says nothing about God not being able to create whatever he wanted. Orderliness in reference to the universe "by definition" could not be univocally applied to God (understood in the classical sense) because "orderliness" concerning the universe means that the parts work together properly. God has no parts (*per* a classical *definition*) and thus such a meaning can't be given to "orderliness" as applied to God.

Next, Whittenberger states, "Finally, morality would not be a 'property' of creation; it would be a product of a creative act of God."[20] There must be a difference between *properties* and *products*. Products are *things* while properties *modify* things. In Aristotelian terms, which is the sense I'm using the terms, a person would be a thing (I guess, product) while a property/accident modifies or qualifies it, such as color, height, or whatever. To say that morality is a product would seem to say that it is a thing in itself. I don't think Whittenberger means that, but it comes across that way. Further, Whittenberger uses the term "property" at various points in the rest of his chapter in reference to morality. In a few paragraphs after this, he says, "In a sense God added a property to himself, and he became perfectly moral."[21] It appears that he is talking about morality being added to God as a property, but he just said morality isn't a property. Furthermore, in chapter 7, Whittenberger said that morality is something created by God.

19. *God, Evil, and Morality*, 80.
20. *God, Evil, and Morality*, 80.
21. *God, Evil, and Morality*, 80.

But that was my point in my argument. In other words, morality is not a necessary feature of God. If Whittenberger wants to maintain that God *became* moral later by adding that property, he needs to give reasons and arguments rather than mere stipulations.

Whittenberger claims that God would want to enter into CUE with humans so he wouldn't be hypocritical.[22] Such is an assertion, not an argument. Further, my argument stating that God doesn't have the property of morality is illustrated in the book of Job. If we replace God's character in the story (and the devil) with humans, most people, if not all, would say that it would be immoral for a human to give permission to kill and cause disease; however, the end of the book offers no such conclusion. The point, agreed on by Job, is that God is not morally unjust *because he is not part of creation*. It is important to point out that every theistic tradition rejects Whittenberger's position. Jews, Muslims, and Christians (until recently) all have historically denied that God is obligated to us.

Whittenberger says, "But after he created CUE he decided to conform to it. CUE specifies how persons should and should not behave with respect to each other. God would conform to his own commands."[23] He decided to conform to it? Where is that stated? God would conform to his own commands? How can Whittenberger know this? Again, this is mere stipulation.

In response to my assertion that Whittenberger's view contradicts aseity since it makes God's goodness dependent and thereby contradicts the "standard definition," he says, "God's aseity would not be changed by having become perfectly moral. He would not be dependent on anything, but he would conform to rules of his own creation. God would not be a hypocrite."[24] However, in such a scenario God's goodness would be dependent on how well he conformed to CUE. Aseity says that God is not dependent on anything for anything. Thus, it really would be a problem for any standard/classical definition to say God is in some way dependent on anything, including CUE. In chapter 5, Whittenberger stated that "if God did exist, his goodness *would be dependent* on what he intends, decides, plans, and does, *just like the goodness of all intelligent agents depend on these things*."[25] Whittenberger definitely thinks that God's goodness *depends* on how he acts. That is perfectly fine, but he will have to abandon the standard

---

22. *God, Evil, and Morality*, 81.
23. *God, Evil, and Morality*, 80.
24. *God, Evil, and Morality*, 81.
25. *God, Evil, and Morality*, 40. Emphasis added.

definition since *any* definition that is allegedly standard or traditional must include divine aseity. However, Whittenberger at least implicitly rejects aseity. My point with all of this is that Whittenberger's case has been to hang his hat on some "standard" definition of God and say we must stick with that. Well, in doing this he is simply rejecting a major tenet of classical theism. He is thus abandoning, implicitly, his definition. But if he is going to abandon it, he must justify why he can abandon it with divine aseity but I can't abandon it (assuming it was part of it) with divine morality.

Another (major) problem with his account of CUE is that while he wants to assert that it is CUE that gives God his moral standing by willingly going along with it, such is really not the case. Whittenberger says that God would not be a hypocrite since he would not give humans moral standards and not agree to the same standards. So, according to Whittenberger, if God created CUE and did not subordinate himself to it like humans, he would be a hypocrite. But being a hypocrite is by anyone's estimation immoral. Whittenberger implies this would be the case in the way he states it. But if God would be immoral by not abiding by CUE, then there must be something that is transcendent over God and CUE. So, it's not really CUE that gives God his moral standing but whatever stands over God and CUE. The problems with this are: (1) a complete lack of acknowledgement of such a moral scheme by Whittenberger; (2) no explanation of where such a moral law comes from or what it even is; (3) why God would be beholden to it; and (4) it would violate many classical doctrines such as aseity and simplicity, thereby violating Whittenberger's standard definition. Bottom line: the standard definition (1) isn't worth very much if so many core doctrines are not part of it, and (2) Whittenberger commits special pleading by picking and choosing which doctrines are and are not part of that standard definition while maintaining that morality must be part of it.

Whittenberger states, "To be beholden to something is not necessarily to be dependent on it. God would be beholden to CUE after he created it, but he would not be dependent on it."[26] To be beholden on something means that there is an obligation: that's what *beholden* means. Further, my quotation of chapter 5 demonstrates that Whittenberger thinks (at least at the writing of that chapter) that God's goodness is dependent on CUE (i.e., he is beholden to it). Thus, aseity is denied.

---

26. *God, Evil, and Morality*, 81.

According to Whittenberger, given God's omniscience and creativity, to include humans, "God would necessarily invent CUE."[27] This is asserted with no argument. Why would God *necessarily* have to create CUE? It seems that latent in Whittenberger's thinking is that God is morally obligated to create it so as to not be a hypocrite.

"I have never endorsed Plato's Forms. Furthermore, moral propositions are neither true nor false. They are prescriptive, not descriptive," Whittenberger declares.[28] I never said that he endorsed the Forms, I was using them to explain aseity. Wouldn't the premises of Whittenberger's arguments be moral propositions? They are certainly talking about harm and suffering and state that God would have a moral obligation to avoid them and be immoral if he didn't. These *propositions* are about God being *moral*. Those sound like moral propositions to me. So, if that is the case, then according to Whittenberger those propositions would not have a truth value. If such were the case, then they would not be relevant to the discussion. However, if Whittenberger retorts that they are not moral propositions, then they still would have no relevance to the discussion since we are talking about God having moral obligations. If his statements aren't about morality, they aren't relevant. Further, prescriptive claims are also truth claims. The claims, "All rocks will sink in water" or "Tylenol helps with headaches" are prescriptive statements, but they are also truth claims. So would the claims of Whittenberger, such as "If God did exist, *then he would* favorably respond to intercessory prayers for healing."[29] According to Whittenberger, such claims have no truth value, so that premise is by definition not true. All of his other arguments have the words "would not have occurred," which are all prescriptive statements. Since sound arguments require the premises to be true, by definition his arguments are not sound (at least according to his logic).

In response to my assertion that he is denying divine simplicity (the notion that there are no parts, properties, or anything within God's nature), he says: "The universe, other persons, and CUE would not be 'created properties,' if God did exist. They would be *products* of his creation! If God did exist, he would have added the properties of 'creator of the universe' and 'perfectly moral' to himself. My understanding of the idea of divine simplicity is that God would not have internal parts; he would not be like a

---

27. *God, Evil, and Morality*, 81-82.
28. *God, Evil, and Morality*, 82.
29. *God, Evil, and Morality*, 24. Emphasis added.

machine. I don't take a position on this hypothesis, but it is not included in the standard definition."[30] In this quote Whittenberger seems to deny that morality is a property (rather, it's a product) and then assert that morality is a *property* ascribed to God. This is a contradiction. Not only does divine simplicity deny internal parts, it rejects the notion of properties, or anything added to God that would modify or change him. He at least takes an implicit position on this by asserting God changes and has properties. While he doesn't understand the doctrine and may not know he's taking a position, he is taking one. To say that simplicity is not part of the standard definition is outrageous. It's outrageous because simplicity has been hailed as the most important doctrine of God from the Middle Ages on, enjoying nearly universal acceptance until just lately. Whittenberger's standard definition is *ad hoc* and question begging. If by "standard" he means "orthodox," then, at least historically speaking, simplicity must be included.

Whittenberger exclaims, "It is not *logically impossible* for a good God to exist! Once again, Huffling is trying to sneak in concepts or terms which I have not used or have discarded."[31] In the context of our discussion, this is exactly what he is saying *given the amount of suffering* (i.e., evil) in the world. In chapter 5 he stated, "It is logically impossible for God to exist and not favorably intervene in response to a request for healing."[32] In other words, unless God is morally good, he can't exist. Since there is so much harm, God can't logically exist. So, given the harm in the world, it is logically impossible, per Whittenberger, that a morally good God exist. Further, Whittenberger said that God takes on morality through creation and CUE. Thus, God wouldn't be morally good before or after creation.

He continues, "Also here, when he talks about a 'greater gain to be had,' he leaves out an essential part of MR#1: '... unless allowing the harm is necessary for producing a greater gain.' Because God would be all-powerful there would be no necessity! For God, the harm would not be necessary for producing a greater gain since he could easily produce whatever gain was to be had without allowing the harm. Theists have ignored this point *ad nauseum*."[33] My point from what was said originally is that Whittenberger would have to know there is no reason for God to allow suffering to happen that would be required for a greater gain. This is evident in the

30. *God, Evil, and Morality*, 82. Emphasis in original.
31. *God, Evil, and Morality*, 84. Emphasis added.
32. *God, Evil, and Morality*, 62.
33. *God, Evil, and Morality*, 84.

context of what I said. To say "Theists have ignored this point *ad nauseum*" demonstrates Whittenberger's complete unfamiliarity with greater-good theodicies, which go back at least to Irenaeus and include many thinkers such as Leibniz, Hick, and Plantinga. My point again: Whittenberger, as a finite being, cannot know that God doesn't allow harm for a greater good. For example, Hick argues that we become better humans via suffering. Leibniz argues for a best-possible-world scenario that requires suffering, and Plantinga argues that if God were to endow humans with the good of free will, he would have to allow the possibility for suffering. Plantinga asserts that even an omnipotent being can't allow free will with no potential for harm.

Whittenberger argues that since "God would be all-powerful, he would not be bound by the 'necessities' by which we are bound."[34] He would seemingly be "bound" by logic in the sense that Plantinga is arguing for. But if God is not "bound by the 'necessities'" that bind us, why should we think he's bound by morality? When I referred to God being "infinite," *contra* Whittenberger, I used the term in reference to (the trait of) knowledge. Further, God being infinite would have to be part of any standard definition, even in regard to his being (it least that's how God is traditionally viewed).

Whittenberger opines that "if God were to allow the Great Tsunami, causing immense harm to human persons, then he would justify to the world why he allowed it. He would present his reasons to the victims, their families and friends, and all of humanity. A moral person doesn't allow harm, when he could stop it, and then not tell others why."[35] (Note this is a prescriptive statement and according to Whittenberger such have no truth value.) I have argued that "Whittenberger aligns himself with the notion that if God exists, he would be a person like humans. This view is known as theistic personalism and is condemned by classical theists."[36] In response, Whittenberger retorts, "I don't know why Huffling keeps harping on this; we have already covered it."[37] (This is ironic since he has covered the standard definition in each chapter.) Unlike Whittenberger et al., I think it's important to emphasize that since God is not a human, we can't expect him to have human qualities.

34. *God, Evil, and Morality*, 84.
35. *God, Evil, and Morality*, 85.
36. *God, Evil, and Morality*, 72.
37. *God, Evil, and Morality*, 85.

Whittenberger claims, "Apparently Huffling fails to accept what most believers already accept—that God would be a person."[38] Such a view is held by theistic personalists, viz., that God and humans are persons in the same way. I deny this, as do classical theists. In fact, in the Christian tradition, God is not seen as *a* person, but three persons in a unified essence. Here, Whittenberger is going against the alleged standard definition (again).

"God would not be exempted from CUE, like President Trump is not exempted from norms, laws, and the constitution," he exhorts.[39] However, President Trump is a human like us, and God is not.

Whittenberger says, "To be a person is to be a moral agent."[40] If this is the case, then God would necessarily be moral by virtue of being a person. However, Whittenberger denies this (sometimes) and says that God took on morality when he decided to follow CUE. He can't have it both ways. Further, is this quote a moral proposition? If so, according to Whittenberger it has no truth value.

He continues, "To assert that God would not be a human is a straw man."[41] Not only is it not a straw man, it is and has been the essence of my argument. My point has been that since God is not a human, he is not bound by human standards. How could such be a straw man?

Whittenberger next states that I have "forgotten or failed to review what [I] actually claimed" regarding my statement that the Bible does not say that God is under some obligation to answer prayer.[42] Of the several passages Whittenberger cites, James would be the most pertinent; however, as already noted, there are various translations and interpretations of this passage. Further, no orthodox position has maintained that God is under any obligation to answer prayer or that he always will, James notwithstanding. In fact, there are many other texts, as mentioned, that state that God will not keep his people from suffering and that suffering is seen as a means to a good end. Again, saying God *would answer prayer* is a prescriptive statement.

In sum, Whittenberger has admittedly refused to debate my central topic, thus, my arguments are not disproven. Further, his arguments are based on moral propositions, but according to him such have no truth

38. *God, Evil, and Morality*, 87.
39. *God, Evil, and Morality*, 87.
40. *God, Evil, and Morality*, 87.
41. *God, Evil, and Morality*, 87.
42. *God, Evil, and Morality*, 87.

value. Thus, since his premises are not true, by definition his arguments are unsound.

11

Summary

GARY J. WHITTENBERGER

BEFORE I SUMMARIZE MY position, I am going to respond to some of the blatant misconceptions in Huffling's chapter 10.

Huffling: "A tsunami causes harm, but Whittenberger is charging God with *evil* in letting it happen. He says God has moral obligations, like humans. What is he charging God with if the notion of evil is off the table?"[1]

Early on in the debate I discarded the concept of "evil" and explained why. I am not charging God with anything! I am concluding that God does not exist. If he did exist, he wouldn't have allowed the Great Tsunami to occur.

Huffling: "I have not violated Ockham's razor as he alleges since I have not multiplied causes needlessly. I am arguing for a transcendent cause of the universe and ironically so did Ockham (he was a theist). Is Whittenberger going to accuse Ockham of violating Ockham's razor?"[2]

If the universe is eternal, which is probably the case, then there would be no cause of it. Huffling and others have invented an unnecessary cause, i.e., God. Yes, Ockham himself violated his own rule!

Huffling: "I care about debunking the false notion that God is a moral being and is required to follow human moral codes."[3]

1. *God, Evil, and Morality*, 91. Emphasis in original.
2. *God, Evil, and Morality*, 92.
3. *God, Evil, and Morality*, 94.

God is a moral being by definition, and Huffgod is an amoral being by definition! I and others have shown that God does not exist. Huffgod very probably does not exist, but that is a topic for another day. God would not be "required to follow human moral codes," but he would choose to abide by CUE, which he would devise by reason.

Huffling: "I have never argued in this debate that a morally good God exists but have consistently maintained no such God exists, which solves the alleged problem of evil (as it is universally called)."[4]

Here Huffling persists in a category error by confusing "god" with "God." Many morally good gods have been proposed, but in this debate I have disputed the existence of only one which happens to be the god believed in by most people in the world. By agreeing that this god does not exist, Huffling has surrendered. He now pledges allegiance to a different god, i.e., Huffgod, which resembles God but is amoral. Although the existence of Huffgod would be compatible with the Great Tsunami, Huffling has not proven that this god exists or why anybody should worship him if he did exist.

Zeus and God are both gods, but they are not the same god, just as Trump and Lincoln were both presidents, but not the same president. Nobody has solved the problem of harm and suffering. And the reason that Huffling has not is because he has engaged in "bait and switch." He substituted Huffgod for God. Whereas Harold Kushner deleted "all-powerful" from the conception of God,[5] Huffling has deleted "perfectly moral," and by doing so they have substituted other gods for God. They violated their god's own First Commandment—"Thou shalt have no other gods before me."

Huffling: "Furthermore, in chapter 7, Whittenberger said that morality is something created by God. But that was my point in my argument. In other words, morality is not a necessary feature of God. If Whittenberger wants to maintain that God *became* moral later by adding that property, he needs to give reasons and arguments rather than mere stipulations."[6]

According to the standard definition, God is perfectly moral, regardless of whether this would be a "necessary feature" or not. It doesn't matter to my argument. I have proposed a sensible way by which God could have become perfectly moral if he did exist. "Perfectly moral" might not

---

4. *God, Evil, and Morality*, 94.
5. Kushner, *When Bad Things Happen*.
6. *God, Evil, and Morality*, 95–96. Emphasis in original.

be a "necessary feature" of God, but it is an essential part of the standard definition.

Huffling: "My point with all of this is that Whittenberger's case has been to hang his hat on some standard definition of God and say we must stick with that. Well, he is simply rejecting a major tenet of classical theism."[7]

The common understanding of God is that he would be perfectly good, benevolent, loving, and/or moral, if he did exist. If he did, then worship of him would be warranted. I suspect that classical theism agrees with me on this, but it is really irrelevant. Some obscure theologians opine that God is amoral, but this is not the common understanding. I am going to stick with what most people have believed about God throughout history. A god who is amoral is not God, but some other fictitious character.

Huffling: "Further, prescriptive claims are also truth claims. The claims, 'All rocks will sink in water' or 'Tylenol helps with headaches' are prescriptive statements, but they are also truth claims."[8]

False. The claims—"All rocks will sink in water" and "Tylenol helps with headaches" are *not* prescriptive statements. They are descriptive statements! Here is a moral prescriptive statement—"One human person should not kill another, except in self-defense." It doesn't describe a state of reality. It is neither true nor false. It states the way persons should not behave. One of the great debates in philosophy has been about the relation of "is" and "ought" statements, but Huffling doesn't seem to see the difference here.

Huffling: "My point again: Whittenberger cannot know as a finite being that God doesn't allow harm for a greater good. For example, Hick argues that we become better humans via suffering. Leibniz argues for a best-possible-world scenario that requires suffering, and Plantinga argues that if God were to endow humans with the good of free will, he would have to allow the possibility for suffering. Plantinga asserts that even an omnipotent being can't allow free will with no potential for harm."[9]

This conclusion shortchanges MR#1. As finite beings we human persons can and do know that if God did exist, he would not allow the Great Tsunami to occur to achieve a greater good because this would be completely unnecessary for an omnipotent being. Hick fails to recognize that if God did exist, he would not create a universe in which human persons

7. *God, Evil, and Morality*, 97.
8. *God, Evil, and Morality*, 98.
9. *God, Evil, and Morality*, 100.

must suffer to "become better humans." A world without great suffering is certainly better than a world with it, so we do not live in the best possible world, as Leibniz thought. Plantinga does not realize that free will is not an all-or-nothing commodity. An omnipotent being could create the free will to engage in some behaviors and not in others. For example, he could make it impossible for persons to freely choose to be aggressive towards others, while allowing them to freely choose between watermelon and cantaloupe at the grocery.

Huffling: "Unlike Whittenberger et al., I think it's important to emphasize that since God is not a human, we can't expect him to have human qualities."[10]

Of course, God would not be a human person! Nobody has said he would be. God and Huffgod are only hypotheticals. They have not been shown to be real things. Most people conceive of God as perfectly moral, and this is why this property is part of the standard definition of God. On the other hand, Huffling conceives of his Huffgod as being amoral. That's fine. Nevertheless, both of these gods are thought to have properties generalized from human persons, just different properties. Human persons live decades long, while these gods are thought to live forever. Human persons have some knowledge, while these gods are thought to have all knowledge which can be had. God is thought to be perfectly moral, while Huffgod is thought to be amoral. Different properties are attributed to different gods, and most of these properties are generalizations or extensions of properties possessed by human beings. After all, the concept of God was created in the image of man.

Huffling: "Again, saying God *would answer prayer* is a prescriptive statement."[11]

False. Huffling confuses "would" with "should." A "should" or "ought" statement is prescriptive, but a "would" statement is not. "Would" describes something if it were to exist.

Huffling: "In sum, Whittenberger has admittedly refused to debate my central topic, thus, my arguments are not disproven. Further, his arguments are based on moral propositions, but according to him such have no truth value. Thus, since his premises are not true, by definition his arguments are unsound."[12]

10. *God, Evil, and Morality*, 100.
11. *God, Evil, and Morality*, 101. Emphasis in original.
12. *God, Evil, and Morality*, 101–102.

In summary, Huffling has failed to find a fatal flaw in any of my four arguments against the existence of God, and so the conclusion of those arguments, i.e., that God does not exist, stands unscathed. Furthermore, I challenged Huffling to focus specifically on my Great Tsunami argument and he never did. In that particular argument neither of the two premises is stated as a "should" statement. Both are true. And the conclusion follows logically from the premises. Huffling's tactic has mostly been "bait and switch." He has pretended to talk about God when he has been talking about Huffgod all along. God does not exist and cannot exist. The existence of God is logically incompatible with the harm and suffering we find in our world. On the other hand, the existence of an amoral god like Huffgod is logically compatible with the harm and suffering we see, but the arguments for this god are weak and it very probably does not exist.

12

Summary

J. Brian Huffling

THE PROBLEM OF EVIL is probably the most common argument against God's existence. Shermer and Whittenberger have argued that evil is evidence against God. While Shermer argues that God *probably* doesn't exist, Whittenberger argues that God *cannot* exist given evil. Both have argued that if God did exist, he would necessarily be a morally perfectly being. Such a position has not been argued for, merely stipulated, especially by Whittenberger. I have argued that God is not the kind of being to be moral since he transcends nature. Since there is nothing that transcends God, he has no standard by which to follow. His goodness, therefore, is not dependent on his actions. In fact, I have been arguing that God's goodness is not moral goodness, but metaphysical goodness. In other words, perfect existence is good in an existential way, but there is no moral connotation from *existence* as such. Moral goodness follows how a being should act based on its nature, such as the human nature. But such a being has an inherent oughtness to fulfill—an oughtness that is programmed by what made that nature. But since God exists on his own and has not been programmed, he has no inherent oughtness.

Why is this relevant? Because the problem of evil (either the logical form or the evidential form) hinges on the notion that if God did exist, he would have an obligation to stop evil from happening. Otherwise, he would be an unjust God and not morally perfect. But if that were the case, then classical theism, so the argument goes, must be false since God is typically defined as a perfectly moral being. So, if God is not perfectly moral, classical theism is false.

But if such an assumption (and it is an assertion—Whittenberger even admits throughout this work that it is merely *stipulated*) is false, then the argument fails. This calls into question the validity of the argument, which is exactly what J. L. Mackie (the famous atheist who popularized the logical form in the mid-twentieth century) said would happen if a premise was called into question. If what I'm saying is true, then God is not obligated to prevent evil and the problem of evil fails.

Most people, atheists as well as theists, look at the "problem" by trying to see how God can exist alongside evil. Atheists say God can't, at least most likely not. Theists say he can and try to give either a theodicy (a justification) or a defense (a way of showing that there is no logical contradiction) before looking at what God is like from positive means. Such a way of looking at this question is backwards. We should not try to deduce what God must be like by fitting him into the problem of evil. God should not be reduced to an answer to such an issue. Rather than trying to retrofit God into the problem of evil, the correct way to examine God's existence and nature is to see if there is any positive evidence for God, and what such evidence may tell us about his nature. It is the nature of God and not just the existence of God that should be examined when dealing with evil. However, God's nature is almost universally ignored in today's discussions of the problem of evil, except to say that he is all-knowing, all-powerful, and all-good. But there are many other and important ways in which the nature of God can inform our discussion.

Another important issue that is often ignored in today's discussion regards the nature of evil. (As stated earlier, while Whittenberger protests the use of the word "evil," this is the universal word used by both theists and atheists. Further, suffering is going to have to be seen as an evil or bad in some way. Further, *evil* is not merely a religious term as he suggests; rather, it has historically been a philosophical issue. However, even given his objection, we should examine the nature of suffering.) If we are going to talk about the problem of *evil*, we have to know what we are talking about. So, we have to look at the existence and nature of God and evil before we can talk about whether they can both "exist" together. With this in mind, let's review the nature of God and evil as I have outlined them and again see how they relate to the so-called problem of evil.

I have provided basic cosmological arguments in this book for God's existence. One such argument is the First Way of Thomas Aquinas. I won't rehearse the argument here since I've already given it, but if sound, it demonstrates that God exists, and exists *in a certain way*. The way in which he exists has a lot to say about how he relates to evil. In short, such (philosophical) arguments demonstrate that God not only exists, but exists as a being of infinite existence, lacking nothing. He is a radically different kind of being from humans. He does not depend on anything. He does not need anything. Such a being is perfect, not in a moral way, but in a sense of *being* with no imperfections. A perfect being cannot get better or improve. This being would (could) not be a moral being in the sense of humans. For humans to be moral means their goodness depends on whether they do the right things that they should do. However, for a completely transcendent being, he has no moral laws that transcend him. His goodness is perfect and does not depend on what he does. No moral imperatives affect him since no other being transcends him. He answers to no one. This is exactly what the story of Job says. After God allowed Satan to kill Job's family and servants and inflict Job with disease, God did not explain how his actions are justified. He doesn't need justifying. He's God. This is basically what Paul says in Romans 9.

This does not beg the question in favor of God in the debate on evil. Rather, we look at the question of God's existence independently of the debate on evil. For, if God does exist, then evil wouldn't magically make him nonexistent. As Brian Davies says, we come to the problem of evil with the "we already know God exists argument." God's existence should be decided before the debate on evil. The theistic proofs for God's existence, if sound, demonstrate a *necessary* being. If so, evil could not *even in principle* negate the existence of a *necessary* being. In short, theists don't have to assume atheism to defend theism. Positive arguments for God are not negated given the existence of evil.

Another point is important in this vein. Atheists bring up evil to theists of all stripes as if evil is a counterexample to their faith. Evil is no surprise to, for example, Jews and Christians. It's part of our religion and worldview. How could something that is part of our own system be an argument *against* our system? Rather than being a counterexample to God's existence, it fits into our belief system very well. We just have an answer to it that atheists simply don't have. In the end, evil will be defeated. So, there is a sense in which the atheist is right: God would want to destroy evil. The atheist just assumes a timetable that is not God's. This is another assumption by the atheist: that they know how God would or should act and even when. God will eliminate evil, just not the way the atheist assumes.

It has been disappointing that Whittenberger has admittedly refused to debate my view of God in this book, saying it is "a topic for another debate."[1] Typically, in debates the opponents debate what the other has argued. But that has not been the case here. Whittenberger has admittedly avoided my arguments that God is not a moral being. But the idea of God being a moral being is a central one for his position. Thus, if he is not a moral being, Whittenberger's case fails. Ultimately, I think Whittenberger's explanation for a transcendent moral code over God fails and is wholly unexplained. Rather, it is *ad hoc*. Further, if, as Whittenberger has said, moral propositions do not have a truth value, then his arguments about God being moral would not be sound since the premises would be moral propositions and would thus have no truth value.

In the end, the problem of evil is not really a problem about God's existence. If God isn't a moral being, then there is no logical impossibility regarding his existence. Further, if God exists, then evil doesn't negate that. Thus, God's existence should be explored via the theistic proofs. God's existence and nature as well as the nature of evil should be explored *before* one declares a problem between them.

---

1. *God, Evil, and Morality*, 79.

PART II

Commentaries on the Debate

13

Commentary from an Atheist

JAMES P. STERBA

THIS BOOK HAD ITS origins in an in-person exchange between Michael Shermer and Brian Huffling in Charlotte, North Carolina which was then captured in contributions they both made to *Skeptic* magazine. At which point, Gary Whittenberger joined the exchange seemingly arguing in support of Shermer's perspective. However, if Whittenberger were actually successful in his attempt to show that the God of traditional theism is logically incompatible with all the significant evil in the world, he would have shown that Shermer was mistaken in his claim that the existence of Christian God was irrefutable. Whittenberger would have succeeded in refuting just the conception of God that Shermer, following Carl Sagan, claimed was irrefutable.

Another anomaly in this exchange is that while both Huffling and Whittenberger report that Shermer's understanding of evil is "intentional harm against sentient beings," Shermer actually endorses a broader conception of evil, claiming that evil is "a descriptive term for a range of environmental events and human behaviors that we describe and interpret as bad, awful, undesirable."[1] It then turns out that Shermer's actual understanding of evil is more similar to Huffling's than to that of Whittenberger who favors limiting evils to moral evils in keeping with the view that both he and Huffling had mistakenly attributed to Shermer. Whittenberger also

---

1. *God, Evil, and Morality*, 9.

ultimately wants to jettison the term "evil" for "morally wrong" thus making his view even further removed from Shermer's view that he claims to be supporting.[2]

Nevertheless, the real story of this book is the seemingly contrasting conceptions of God presented by Huffling and Whittenberger respectively. Whittenberger's conception sees God as morally good, whereas Huffling claims that God is good but not morally good. Whittenberger thinks that he has shown that the God who fits his conception is logically incompatible with the horrendous evil in the world. Huffling thinks his own conception of God is able to avoid the fate of Whittenberger's conception. Huffling also complains, with some justification, that Whittenberger fails to sufficiently attend to the conception of God that Huffling actually defends, preferring instead to argue against the conception of God as morally good that Whittenberger himself puts forward for the purpose of critiquing it.

But what is Whittenberger's argument against God understood to be morally good that he claims refutes that conception of God? Whittenberger actually has two versions: Both address the evils of the 2004 Tsunami in Southeast Asia, the Holocaust, and rapes generally. In the first version, Whittenberger argues that God being perfectly moral "would not intentionally create conditions that cause harm to other beings," if he "could avoid it, and he could avoid it because he would be all-powerful."[3] In the second version, Whittenberger puts forward the following moral rule: "Person X should prevent harm to person Y, if he is able, unless allowing the harm is necessary for producing a greater gain and X also justifies this exception."[4] This rule introduces the possibility of exceptions based on greater gain, a possibility not included in the first version of Whittenberger's argument. Yet while introducing the possibility of exceptions into his second version of his argument, Whittenberger never considers whether his own examples of horrendous evils might be just such exceptions to his rule. Instead, he simply assumes, without argument, that an all-powerful God could secure greater gains without doing or permitting any significant evil.

But this is a mistake. There are goods, for example, consoling a rape victim, that even an all-powerful God could not secure without doing or permitting significant evil, for example, in this case, permitting a rape. Accordingly, in order for Whittenberger's argument to work, he must show

2. *God, Evil, and Morality*, 35.
3. *God, Evil, and Morality*, 22.
4. *God, Evil, and Morality*, 58.

that there are no goods that are logically dependent on the existence of the evils he cites, goods that would serve to justify God permitting those evils. Whittenberger has not done this.[5] Thus, although Whittenberger may be able to justifiably claim that it is unlikely that there are such goods, to have a successful *logical* argument from evil against the existence of an all-good, all-powerful God of traditional theism, he would need to show that it is *logically impossible* for there to be such goods, and this is something that Whittenberger never even attempted to do.

But is Huffling any better off? Huffling claims that by denying that God is morally good, he has eliminated one of the premises that is needed for a logical argument against the existence of God that Whittenberger mistakenly claims to have provided. But even if Huffling had succeeded in doing this, he would still need a justification for dropping the assumption that God is morally good. Here is an argument that Huffling repeats twice in support of dropping that assumption.

1. If God is the creator of the universe, then he does not have properties of creation.
2. Morality is a property of creation.
3. Therefore, God does not have moral properties—he is not a moral being.[6]

To evaluate Huffling's argument, let's keep the first premise and substitute for the second "Intelligence is a property of creation." Now Huffling does not want to draw the conclusion that God does not have the property of intelligence—that he is not an intelligent being. In fact, in chapter 5 Huffling affirms that intelligence is an analogical property possessed by both God and ourselves. Here is his general view about such predications:

> My position is that God is analogous with respect to certain descriptions of humans, not univocal to them. For example, since humans and God do not have knowledge the same way, they have knowledge in an analogous way.[7]

---

5. Whittenberger holds that God created the moral standard before he created other persons, but a far better position for atheists to defend is to hold that moral standards, like the standard of logic, are not made by God but are rather independent of God and us.
6. *God, Evil, and Morality*, 15, 68.
7. *God, Evil, and Morality*, 72.

In addition, elsewhere Huffling affirms that God is rich in mercy toward us, that he loves us, and that he is virtuous, all of which are to be understood to be analogical properties possessed by both God and ourselves.[8] So, Huffling provides no reason for not taking "morally good" to be an analogous predication of God just like the other traits Huffling recognizes as analogous predications of God. In fact, in chapter 10, Huffling allows that God is morally good, but not "in the way that humans are," which is just the way Huffling describes the analogous predication of knowledge in the passage quoted above.[9]

Accordingly, Huffling has not really given up the assumption that God is morally good but rather has understood that such predications apply analogously to ourselves and to God, just the way Aquinas and other medievals had understood them.[10] Still, in order for God to be morally good in this way, it would have to be the case that the kinds and amounts of evil that God would be permitting in the world would be logically necessary to achieve greater goods that would serve to justify them. This is how God needs to be defended against the logical problem of evil. But Huffling does not do this. The only kind of defense of God against the problem of evil that Huffling provides is not really a defense at all but simply a roundabout way of claiming that predications apply to God analogously to the way they apply to us. But the kind of defense of God against the logical problem of evil that is needed, one that shows that the kinds and amounts of evil that God would be permitting in the world are logically necessary to achieve greater goods that would serve to justify them, Huffling does not even attempt to provide.

It also should be noted that Huffling in an earlier response to a similar critique I make of his view spends some time showing how intelligence is predicated differently of God than ourselves, but then concludes with: "So, it is proper to say that God is intelligent, but the kind of intelligence is only analogous to ours and is unique to his being."[11] But that is just what, I have

8. Huffling, "God is Not a Moral Being."
9. *God, Evil, and Morality*, 89.
10. McInerny, *Aquinas and Analogy*.
11. See Huffling's "Is God Morally Obligated" and my "Sixteen Contributors," both appeared in 2021 in "Is the God of Traditional Theism Logically Compatible with All the Evil in the World?" This was a special issue in *Religions* for which I was the special editor. See also Huffling's "The Problem of Evil and God's Moral Standing" which appeared in 2023 in "Do We Now Have a Logical Argument from Evil," another special in *Religions* for which I am also the special editor. My response to Huffling and the other thirty-nine contributors to this special issue should be published soon.

argued, Huffling should say about God's being morally good, and for the same reasons. Hence, Huffling has not escaped the charge of special pleading as he had hoped to do.

It is also important to realize that Huffling and Whittenberger are really talking not about two different conceptions of God, as initially seemed to be the case, but rather they are really talking about the same conception of the God of traditional theism. Once Huffling's claim that "God is good but not morally good" is unpacked to mean that "God is good but not morally good in the same way we are morally good but only analogously so" Whittenberger has no reason not to accept the same conception of the God that Huffling endorses. Unfortunately, while sharing the same conception of the God of traditional theism, Huffling and Whittenberger also share a common failure to meet their opposing argumentative goals. Thus, Huffling fails to show that the kinds and amounts of evil that God would be permitting in the world are logically necessary to achieve greater goods that would serve to justify them, and Whittenberger fails to show that there are no goods that are logically dependent on the existence of the evils he cites which would serve to justify God permitting those evils. Of course, both Huffling and Whittenberger could not have been both successful in their opposing quests, but was it necessary that they both fail in those quests as well?

Now some theists have argued that the opportunity to be friends with God is the greatest good we could receive, and that our receiving that good would more than compensate for all horrendous evil consequences that have occurred in the world. Yet the God of traditional theism could not be logically constrained to permit such horrendous evil consequences before he could offer us the opportunity to be friends with himself. Otherwise, he would not be all-powerful, and hence, not the God of traditional theism. Hence, theism cannot be defended in this way. Hence, God could have provided us with the opportunity to be friends with himself without permitting all the horrendous evil consequences that occur in the world, but clearly any God that exists has not done this.[12]

Yet isn't it possible that there are other goods that are logically dependent on God's permitting horrendous evil consequences that are logically connected to God's permission of those consequences that would serve to

---

12. Of course, we would not have been born (naturalistically) except for the evil consequences that have occurred in the world. Nevertheless, neither God nor we are under any obligation to permit horrendous evil consequences in order to bring possible people (us before we come into the world) into existence.

justify God's permission of those consequences? Even if theists, like Huffling, cannot show that there are such goods and so secure a proof that the all-good all-powerful God of traditional theism would still exist given all the horrendous evil consequences in the world, atheists, like Whittenberger, may still be able to provide a proof that there are no such goods logically dependent on the existence of such horrendous evil consequences that would serve to justify God's permission of such consequences. Let's explore whether that can be done.

To secure such a proof we would need to first provide a way of capturing all the goods that God could provide to us.

Here it is important to see that goods that could be provided to us are of just two types. Either they are goods to which we have a right or they are goods to which we do not have a right. That captures all the goods that could be provided to us. In addition, goods to which we are entitled and goods to which we are not entitled are either first-order goods, like the freedom not to be brutally assaulted, that do not logically presuppose that any serious wrong has occurred or second-order goods, like receiving needed medical aid after having been brutally assaulted, that do logically presuppose that some serious wrongdoing has occurred.[13]

FIRST-ORDER GOODS TO WHICH WE HAVE A RIGHT

Now for all first-order goods to which we have a right, the basic moral requirement that governs their provision is:

Moral Evil Prevention Requirement A[14]

> Prevent rather than permit especially the horrendous evil consequences of immoral actions (a good to which we have a right) when, without violating anyone's rights, that can easily be done. And no other good or goods are at stake.

---

13. For X to logically presuppose Y here and similarly for X to logically depend on Y means that it is not logically possible for X to obtain without Y also obtaining.

14. In earlier work I referred to Moral Evil Requirement I–III. Moral Evil Requirement A-C are those same requirements placed in a slightly different order for reasons of exposition.

With respect to first-order goods to which we have a right, we are sometimes stuck in a situation where we can only provide some people with such a good and hence prevent a corresponding evil from being inflicted on them by not providing other people with another good whose nonprovision inflicts a lesser evil on them. For example, we may only be able to save five people from being robbed and viciously assaulted who are close by if we don't try to also save two other people from being robbed and viciously assaulted who are farther away. God, however, would never find himself causally stuck in such situations. God would always have the causal power to prevent both evils and would be required to do so given that it is assumed that no other good or goods are at stake.

Now MEPR A is supposed to be an exceptionless (necessary) moral requirement. Consider what it claims put colloquially: *Prevent horrendous evil consequences when one can easily do so without violating anyone's rights and no other goods are at stake.* What is there not to like about that requirement? How can it not be a necessary moral requirement?

GOODS TO WHICH WE DO NOT HAVE A RIGHT

With respect to goods to which we do not have a right, not providing such goods to others, even when we could easily do so, is not morally evil. Not providing such goods to would-be beneficiaries would not be a way of wronging them. In any case, such goods are also either first-order goods that do not logically depend on serious wrongdoing, like many of the friendships we have, or second-order goods that do logically depend on the occurrence of any serious wrongdoing, like the opportunity to provide medical care to someone who has been brutally assaulted. Now for all such first-order goods to which we do not have a right, the basic moral requirement that governs the provision of them is:

Moral Evil Prevention Requirement B

> Do not permit rather than prevent especially the horrendous evil consequences of immoral actions (which would violate someone's rights) in order to provide would-be recipients with goods to which they do not have a right that are not logically dependent on God's permission of those consequences, thus making them

first-order goods, when there are countless morally unobjectionable ways of providing those goods.

FIRST-ORDER GOODS TO WHICH WE DO NOT HAVE A RIGHT

Now with respect to first-order goods to which we do not have a right, both God and we would have numerous ways of providing people with such goods without violating anyone's rights by permitting rather than preventing especially the horrendous evil consequences of immoral actions to be inflicted on them. In cases where we humans are causally constrained by lack of resources and are thus unable to provide someone with such a good without permitting the violation of the person's rights, God would never be subject to such causal constraints.

Of course, it might be objected here that, for all we know, it could just be logically impossible for God to both provide us with first-order goods to which we do not have a right and to prevent horrendous evil consequences of immoral actions from being inflicted on us, something to which we do have a right. Again, this seems to be something that skeptical theists might want to say. But as these goods have been specified, they are first-order goods to which we do not have a right. Being such first-order goods, their provision does not logically depend on occurrence of any previous wrongdoing that God would have to have permitted. Hence, it would be logically possible for God to both provide us with such first-order goods to which we do not have a right while preventing horrendous evil consequences of immoral actions from being inflicted on us, something to which we do have a right. And this undercuts the objection that there are no goods that are logically dependent on the existence of the evils he cites, goods that would serve to justify God permitting those evils.

Therefore, it must be the case that God can both provide us with first-order goods to which we do not have a right and prevent especially the horrendous evil consequences of immoral actions from being inflicted on us, something to which we do have a right.[15] That being the case, there are no grounds at all for making the provision of first-order goods to which we do not have a right conditional upon God's not preventing especially

---

15. Sometimes I am assuming a conclusive right as here. At other times, as the "not having a right" in the next sentence, I am assuming just *prima facie* right.

horrendous evil consequences of immoral actions from being inflicted on us, given that we have a right to that prevention by whomever is in a position to do so without violating anyone's rights. Thus, suppose God were to permit the horrendous consequences of a vicious assault to be inflicted on two victims to provide them with the opportunity to be good friends with each other. That opportunity to be good friends with each other is a good that is not logically dependent on God's permission of the assault (God could have provided them with the opportunity to be good friends without permitting them to be assaulted) and so that good belongs to the domain of MEPR B.

Now MEPR B is supposed to be an exceptionless (necessary) moral requirement. Consider what it claims. Put colloquially, it says: *Don't secure a good using morally objectionable means when you can easily secure the same good by using morally unobjectionable means*. What then is there not to like about this requirement? How could anyone object to it?

SECOND-ORDER GOODS TO WHICH WE HAVE A RIGHT

Now with respect to second-order goods to which we have a right, like the good of life-saving medical aid after one has been brutally assaulted, it would be wrong not to provide such goods when one can easily do so without violating anyone's rights. However, given that the need we have for such goods depends on the occurrence of serious moral wrongdoing, it would be morally required for anyone who could easily do so without violating anyone's rights to prevent the consequences of that wrongdoing on which the second-order good depends. Hence, the victims of horrendous moral wrongdoing who would have a second-order right to such goods would have morally preferred that anyone who could easily have done so without violating anyone's rights would have kept them from suffering the consequences of the wrongdoing that would ground their right to any second-order goods of rectification and compensation. For example, a victim of a vicious assault would have morally preferred that anyone who could easily have done so without violating anyone's rights would have prevented the consequences of his assault to his now having the right to second-order goods resulting from that assault. So, we have:

Moral Evil Prevention Requirement C

> Do not permit rather than prevent the infliction of especially horrendous evil consequences of immoral actions on their would-be victims in order to provide would-be beneficiaries with goods they would morally prefer not to have.[16]

SECOND-ORDER GOODS TO WHICH WE DO NOT HAVE A RIGHT

The very possibility of second-order goods to which we do not have a right is conditional on the occurrence of a moral wrongdoing. For example, consider the opportunity to console a rape victim. No one is entitled to be provided with such a good, and its very existence depends upon God's permission of a rape. Hence, it would be morally required for anyone who could do so without violating anyone's rights to prevent the consequences of the rape on which the second-order good of the opportunity to console the rape victim depends. Thus, the would-be beneficiaries would morally prefer not to be implicated in the violation of people's fundamental rights which would obtain if they accepted such goods, given that they can easily do without them while still enjoying the opportunity to be friends with God, the resources for a decent life, and an equal liberty for soul-making and given that they don't need and can easily do without the goods that are logically dependent on those evil consequences. Thus, God should have acted to respect their moral preferences not to receive such goods. Even the perpetrators of such wrongful deeds, who later have the opportunity to repent and seek forgiveness would always morally prefer that God had prevented the consequences of their immoral deeds. So, in virtue of MEPR C, God should have acted to respect the moral preferences of all those who are the beneficiaries of the horrendous evil consequences of immoral actions and prevented their infliction.

So, what about MEPR C? Is it not on a par with MEPR A and B as a necessary moral requirement? In the case of MEPR C, preventing the horrendous evil consequences does not provide the only good that is at stake for the would-be beneficiaries, as is the case for MEPR A. Nor is it the case

---

16. A moral preference here is a preference that it would be morally wrong not to have.

for MEPR C that the would-be beneficiaries could get whatever good is at issue without permitting horrendous evil consequences as holds for MEPR B. Rather, for MEPR C, the goods that would-be beneficiaries could receive if God were to prevent the horrendous evil consequences at issue are just incomparably greater than the goods that they could receive if God permitted those horrendous evil consequences, and this holds especially for those on whom the horrendous evil consequences would have been inflicted if God permitted them. Hence, there is no way the moral argument for the requirements of MEPR C could be any stronger.

In sum, all goods that could be provided to us are either goods to which we have a right or goods to which we do not have a right. Each of these types further divides into first-order goods that do not logically depend on moral wrongdoing and second-order goods that do logically depend on moral wrongdoing. With respect then to first-order goods to which we have a right and first-order goods to which we do not have a right, MEPR A and B respectively morally constrain the pursuit of greater-good justifications for both God and us. And with respect to second-order goods to which we have a right and second-order goods to which we do not have a right, according to MEPR C the preferences of the would-be beneficiaries of such goods morally require that God prevent the first-order evil consequences on which the very existence of those second-order goods depend.

As noted, before, to meet his argumentative goal, Whittenberger needed to show that there are no goods that are logically dependent on the existence of the evils which he cites that would serve to justify God permitting those evils.

I have now met that goal. I have recognized that there are goods that are logically dependent on the existence of the evil consequences that Whittenberger cites. Yet crucially I have also used MEPR A-C to show that those goods would not serve to justify God permitting those evil consequences. MEPR A and B are just no-brainer requirements, and for MEPR C, the goods that would-be beneficiaries could receive if God were to prevent the horrendous evil consequences at issue are just incomparably greater than the goods that they could receive if God permitted those horrendous evil consequences. That constitutes a conclusive argument showing that the analogously all-good, all-powerful God of traditional theism that Huffling wanted to defend and Whittenberger wanted to critique is logically incompatible especially with all the horrendous evil consequences in the world.

Of course, my argument does not rule out the possibility of there being a "god" not all-good and/or not all-powerful who is the cause of the universe. Yet given all the horrendous evil in the world that should have been prevented, such a "god" would have to be either extremely immoral, more immoral than all of our historical villains taken together whose horrendous evil consequences he would have permitted, or, while morally good, such a "god" would have to be extremely weak, not being able to prevent those horrendous evil consequences in the world that should have been prevented. It is doubtful, however, that either Huffling or Whittenberger would be interested in exploring this "god" possibility further.

14

Commentary from a Theist

RICHARD G. HOWE

FOR MILLENNIA, THINKERS HAVE been reflecting upon and arguing about the reasonableness of believing in the existence and goodness of God or gods in light of the presence of evil in the world. We can thank—or curse as the case may be—David Hume for resurrecting the ancient formulation of the "problem of evil" from the ancient writer Lactantius.[1] The historical form of the problem has been modified or augmented by some as a number of philosophical voices have joined the conversation over the centuries. An important aspect of such modifications or augmentations is that it allows the debate to expand over a larger field of the relevant philosophical issues. For example, Lactantius's simpler version does not consider the epistemological side of the question. Asking whether the God of Christianity could

1. Lactantius (240–320) was one of a group of Latin apologists which also included Tertullian (160–225). Frederick Copleston comments that "the origin of the soul by God's direct creation, in opposition to any form of traducianism, was clearly affirmed by Lactantius." Copleston, *A History of Philosophy*, 25. As a matter of historical interest, in David Hume's *Dialogues Concerning Natural Religion*, the interlocutor Philo (presumably the "voice" of Hume) credits Epicurus with the oft-quoted formulation of the problem of evil (See Hume, *Dialogues*, 84). It would seem that Hume is actually quoting Lactantius (240–320), who is himself crediting Epicurus with the formulation. Every internet search I have done that credits the origin of the formulation credits it to Epicurus. But I have never found any such reference give any citation to any writing of Epicurus. Arizona State University philosophy professor Thomas A. Blackson comments that "there is little reason to think that Epicurus actually gave this particular argument." Blackson, "Epicureanism."

have known in advance whether his free creatures would perpetrate any evil brings into the conversation additional offerings of solutions, including Molinism and open theism. Given that Huffling, as a Thomist,[2] rejects on metaphysical grounds the plausibility of either Molinism or open theism, it is not surprising that these "solutions" do not enter into the conversation. It surely would have been a waste of time and effort to try to critique an option with which the Christian was not sympathetic.[3]

SOME THOUGHTS ON THE CONVERSATION

I would now like to make some comments on the conversation. My comments will be a mix of observations and evaluation of certain points that were made by the participants, together with a few points of my own. My comments will generally follow the order in which the points were made by the interlocutors.

Some Thoughts on Michael Shermer

Not surprisingly, Shermer tees up his argument against God by rehearsing dire statistics showing just how bad the world actually is; as if the fact of evil was itself in dispute. I fear that the attempt here is to generate enough of an emotional response so that the momentum of these emotions can carry the reader over to Shermer's "solution" (i.e., that God does not exist), thereby

---

2. The philosophy (particularly the metaphysics) of Thomas Aquinas (1225–74) arises largely from the philosophy of Aristotle (384–322 BC) with certain influences from Neoplatonism. Aquinas's most important augmentation of Aristotle's metaphysics has to do with how Aquinas understood existence.

3. For a short treatment defending Molinism, see Craig, *The Only Wise God*. Craig also has numerous video lectures and some debates on the internet dealing with Molinism. For a treatment of open theism vis-à-vis the problem of evil, see Boyd, *God of the Possible*, 98–103. The reader should interpret all of my comments about what I think the "Christian" God is like in the context of me being a Thomist, as is Brian Huffling. This is vitally important to the discussion since employing the metaphysics of Aquinas (particularly within the camp of the existential Thomism of Etienne Gilson, Joseph Owens, and others) has everything to do with how the issue of the problem of evil should be framed and addressed. Granted, Thomism is a minority view in contemporary Protestant Christianity. Even more, most of the contemporary evangelical Christian philosophers with whom I am familiar are not sympathetic to Thomism. A sampling of some evangelical Christian philosophers who are Thomists would include: Dolezal, *All That Is in God*; Geisler, *Systematic Theology*; and Haines, *Natural Theology*.

alleviating some burden that his argument would otherwise need to shoulder. Ironically it seems to me, the majority of people I have encountered or about whom I have read who have personally experienced much suffering and evil have not at all moved towards atheism as a means of "explaining" what is happening to them.[4] To be sure, the atheist might have an explanation of this phenomenon (e.g., that such people are "wishing" there is a God who someday will deliver them from their plight, if in no other sense, at least in heaven after they die). In this case, the atheist will have to revert back to the philosophical and theological arguments themselves when the stark reality of evil fails to carry the day with an audience.

Shermer says, "Claims that cannot be tested, assertions immune to disproof are veridically worthless . . . . What I'm asking you to do comes down to believing, in the absence of evidence, on my say-so."[5] The reader should note that Shermer, in the context of insisting that the Christian offer evidence for his or her claim that God exists and is good even in light of the evil in the world, conspicuously offers no evidence for his own claim that "claims that cannot be tested, assertions immune to disproof are veridically worthless." Am I allowed to insist that Shermer offers evidence for this claim? In the absence of any evidence from him, should the reader conclude that Shermer's claim is "veridically worthless"? Exactly what could such evidence look like? The problem is (as is evidenced by his dragon example) the principle of falsifiability, by and large, only applies to physical claims. Any criteria of falsifiability for philosophical claims (as this claim by Shermer is) will look very different than those for physical claims. Huffling rightly points out that, given this broader notion of falsifiability, the Christian theist's claims about God can be falsified by, for example, showing how such claims are logically impossible. Since, as Huffling has pointed out, atheists admit that the logical problem of evil is a failure, then Shermer's raising the specter of falsifiability is a non-starter.[6] Thus, it would seem that Shermer

---

4. Though my life has not been fraught with overmuch evil and suffering as many have endured, I vividly remember how "close to God" (to use a Christian expression) I "felt" (for lack of a better term here) despite going through the pain of the passing of my father when he was at the young age of sixty-five. I am not denying that there are those for whom the personal problem of evil has moved them towards atheism. But this reinforces the point that rehearsing such dire statistics, as is sometimes the case in this discussion, fails to serve a given conclusion or solution to the problem.

5. *God, Evil, and Morality*, 6.

6. To be fair, not every atheist has given up on the logical problem of evil. See for example, Sterba, *Is a Good God Logically Possible?* Commenting upon Sterba's argument, atheist Richard Carrier concludes, "So as clever and useful I find Sterba's argument to be,

has set up the wrong "test" for ascertaining whether it is reasonable to believe that the Christian God exists given the evil in the world.

What, then, should any test be like? As Huffling demonstrates several times, the argument has to employ questions in philosophy, particularly metaphysics. He is certainly right when he says, "discussions about God and evil are inherently philosophical in nature."[7] This undoubtedly puts the conversation onto a plane that is off-putting if not inaccessible to many. It certainly poses a challenge to make a sufficient attempt to build a philosophical argument within a limited context or theatre of conversation. Further, it sets some Christians against other Christians regarding how to best respond to the critics, since one will find basic philosophical differences within Christianity. But it is unavoidable that the conversation engages philosophy. With Huffling, it is my contention as well that we can know God exists and that God has a number of attributes (including goodness) antecedent to, and irrespective of, any acquaintance of evil in this world. Because Shermer is innocent of how the Thomist might argue given the opportunity to make the case more thoroughly, many of his responses are irrelevant to the classical theism of Aquinas.[8]

This is no more evident when Shermer says to Huffling, "I'd like to steel man your argument but I honestly have no idea what your position is." Shermer goes on, "Can you just explain to me please, why God does not cure childhood leukemia?"[9] The problem here is that Shermer thinks the reasonableness of concluding that the Christian God is good depends upon the cogency of one's answer to this question (and perhaps many like it). That is why Shermer thinks he has exposed something important when Huffling answers the question with "I don't know." In other words, in Shermer's view unless one can give a reasonable answer to the question, the

---

I don't see it providing a logical proof of the impossibility of a good God." Carrier, "Is a Good God Logically Possible?" Other atheists who concur that the logical problem of evil fails include: Mackie, *The Miracle of Theism*, 154; Martin, *Atheism*, 335; and Weisberger, "The Argument from Evil," 167.

7. *God, Evil, and Morality*, 11.

8. It is challenging to discuss the "Christian" God inasmuch as Christian philosophers differ on some of the philosophical technicalities of God's nature. The most conspicuous debate today is between classical theism and theistic personalism. Huffling (as am I) is a classical theist. He succinctly lists some of the characteristics of classical theism. Note that the monikers are not used consistently. What is more, as is the case of many labels, the labels are given to a viewpoint by its detractors. This is the case with "theistic personalism." Many in that camp reject the label.

9. *God, Evil, and Morality*, 9.

best position to take is that the Christian God does not exist. But for the classical theist, the answer to the question of whether the Christian God is good is entailed necessarily by the metaphysical commitments that classical theism takes. Thus, what is needed is a conscientious examination of the metaphysics. But instead of getting that, Shermer responds with "If the only answer—no matter how loaded with philosophical jargon it is—comes down to 'God works in mysterious ways' and 'who can understand God?' you don't have a case."[10] In addition to the fallacious *ad hominem* pejorative "philosophical jargon" expression, Shermer is apparently quite unaware that the classical theist's solution to the problem of evil—even if one accepted the characterization "God works in mysterious ways"—has nothing to do with the conclusion that God is good. That conclusion is entailed by the antecedent philosophy (metaphysics) of the classical theist. Perhaps that philosophy is wrong. If Shermer thinks it is wrong, he never tells us why, despite his claim that he has "read all the arguments trying to square the circle of evil." He merely contemptuously characterizes any attempt as "philosophical jargon."

What is needed is the best demonstration that can be made that the Christian God is good. But what this demonstration (or argument) will look like will be very different depending upon whether the Christian making the argument engages with the philosophical aspects of the issue and whether his or her philosophical orientation is along the lines of contemporary analytic philosophy or a more classical philosophy. Huffling did a herculean job of laying out the case from the position of classical theism when managing such a robust topic as the problem of evil within the constraints of a conversational exchange.

Some Thoughts on Gary Whittenberger

In my experience, people today confine the use of the term "evil" to moral evil. In contrast, events that might cause damage or suffering, while called "bad" or "undesirable" or some other related term, are seldom if ever called "evil." This distinction arises from contemporary philosophers who catalog evil as "natural evil" (unwarranted suffering caused by unconscious natural forces) or "moral evil" (unwarranted suffering caused by persons). The term "evil" in the popular usage became confined to the latter. No doubt this contributes to some confusion when confronted with a classical philosopher in

10. *God, Evil, and Morality*, 10.

the tradition of Augustine and Aquinas for whom "evil" refers to any sort of depravation in a thing.[11] As Huffling pointed out, the notion of depravation presupposes a notion of what the thing "ought" to be. A human who cannot see is suffering a privation since, by virtue of being a human, the human *ought* to see. This is an example of an evil. In contrast, a rock, which also cannot see, does not have a privation since it is not of the nature of a rock to see.

Here, then, is another potentially confusing term for the contemporary debate. Just as "evil" is almost always thought of in moral terms, sometimes the term "ought" is thought of in moral terms. Other times "ought" is used in a prudential way (e.g., "If you want to arrive at this particular destination, then you *ought* to take this particular route").

Despite Huffling's efforts, Whittenberger seems to continue to misunderstand Huffling's use of the term "evil" and accuses him of being inconsistent. I suspect my efforts to sort things out for him will be equally unsuccessful. But I should like to remind the reader that Huffling is arguing that the classical notion of evil as a depravation presupposes that things have natures (sometimes the term "essence" is used) which constitute what they are and what properties ("accidents" in classical terminology) a given thing ought to have by virtue of being that thing. To be sure, these points employ the metaphysics of Aristotle (notably his ten categories)[12] together with the augmentations of Aquinas, most importantly his notion of existence[13] and his notion of the analogy of language.[14] Huffling repeatedly seeks to alert his interlocutors that the philosophy of the issue is of paramount importance. A scrupulous treatment of the problem of evil requires the engagement of sound philosophy.

To be sure, such philosophical notions of Aquinas are debatable. They occasion rigorous debate even among Christian—indeed, evangelical—philosophers. But rarely does the contention between the atheist and the Christian deal with the issues at that level when it comes to the classical

---

11. Augustine says that "evil is only the privation of a good." *Confessions* III, 7, §12. Aquinas says, "Evil is simply a privation of something which a subject is entitled by its origin to possess and which it ought to have." *Summa Contra Gentiles*, III, 7, §2.

12. See Aristotle, *Categories*, 1b25–2a4.

13. See Aquinas, *On Being and Essence*.

14. It is a challenge that Aquinas does not deal with the analogy of language in one place. Rather, his discussion of it is spread throughout his voluminous writings. Good secondary sources would include: Klubertanz, *St. Thomas Aquinas on*; Rocca, *Speaking the Incomprehensible God*; and Coté, "Truth's Light and Supereminent Darkness."

(i.e., Thomistic) understanding of God.[15] This ends up making many of the criticisms the atheist might level completely miss their mark.

This is no better illustrated than by Whittenberger when he enthusiastically "agrees" with Huffling in saying, "Of course we don't have knowledge of what God is, i.e., what his nature is, since we don't even know that God exists!"[16] Because Whittenberger seemingly is innocent of any acquaintance with Aquinas's doctrine of analogy (or, for that matter with the Aristotelian/Thomistic position on human knowing), he misses the significance of what it means in this tradition to say that we do not know God's nature.[17] I am not saying that if only critics like Shermer and Whittenberger understood Aquinas, they would agree with Aquinas's views. Instead, I am saying that if critics like Shermer and Whittenberger understood Aquinas and still rejected his views, it would be for entirely different reasons than the ones they give.

The value of an appeal to these philosophical tenets regarding the nature of evil itself, and its connection to moral evil and the problem of evil, is that, as a subset of a broader issue, it can lead to an exploration of how one should define the term "God." Whittenberger does a fair job of laying out an array of attributes that he is confident is "the god [sic] believed in by my most Jews, Christian, and Muslims."[18] I have seen no polls, so I cannot comment whether it is true that his list of attributes is indeed held by most in these religions. I do think, however, that the classical theism that Huffling is championing has a significant history with formidable thinkers championing this classical theism within each of these traditions. Regrettably, the contours of this history are lost on much of the contemporary conversations. That classical theism has a long history is not a proof that it is true. But the fact that the contours of the history of this same classical theism are lost on much of the contemporary conversations is not a proof that it is false.

But one major problem lurking underneath much of the conversation is the temptation to regard the question of God's existence and nature on

---

15. A read through *The Cambridge Companion to Atheism* edited by the atheist philosopher Michael Martin will show a dearth of adequate interaction with the luminaries of classical theism, whether Jewish (e.g., Maimonides), Christian (e.g., Aquinas), or Islamic (e.g., Ibn Sina).

16. *God, Evil, and Morality*, 34.

17. For a treatment of the Thomistic model of human knowing see: Owens, *Cognition* and Wilhelmsen, *Man's Knowledge of Reality*.

18. *God, Evil, and Morality*, 21.

par in principle with questions about other things in reality. Whether it is debates about the existence of UFOs or Sasquatch or the Loch Ness Monster or stockpiles of weapons of mass destruction in some foreign country or the gods of other religions, the typical format is that the one making the claim offers "evidence" supporting the claim and, when warranted, the one denying the claim offers "evidence" countering the claim. Thus, we move from one item to another item debating whether a given thing has existence or not. The challenge of the Thomist is in attempting to convey to the critic that the God of classical theism is not some "thing" in reality that has existence. Instead, the claim is that God *is* subsistent existence itself. The God of classical theism is not a thing that "has" certain attributes that distinguish it to some extent from other things. It is not that there are countless "gods" out there and that the classical theist is vying to convince others that his particular "god" is the only one that exists. Rather, the classical theist in the tradition of Augustine and Aquinas is claiming that God is *self-existing being itself*.[19]

Clearly, this characterization that Huffling has touched upon is pregnant with philosophical assumptions. It is precisely due to these assumptions that the case for the existence and nature of God arises. These assumptions might be true or they might be false. But it will not do for the atheist to frame the discussion in the absence of the philosophical foundation undergirding the case for the God of classical Christianity and then expect the classical theist to nevertheless make his or her case.

Because it sometimes takes so much philosophical backfilling to make his case clear to his critics, invariably a classical theist like Huffling will have to revert to the more standard theistic arguments given in the contemporary debate. Such arguments have the advantage of requiring less philosophical knowledge of the hearer. But they have the disadvantage of not delivering enough of the classical attributes of the God. One common argument is the kalam, which Huffling gives. I use this argument as well.[20]

19. There are many good treatments of Aquinas's theistic arguments, including: Kerr, *Aquinas's Way to God* and Knasas, *Thomistic Existentialism and Cosmological Reasoning*.

20. This is one place where I philosophically disagree with Aquinas. He maintained that this argument was not sound. In other words, Aquinas argued that the kind of infinite which this argument employs cannot show whether or not the universe began to exist at some point in the past. Aquinas sharply distinguishes the infinite of the kalam with the impossibility of the infinite in the first three of his five ways. For an explanation of the differences and the difference it makes in the theistic arguments, see Howe, "Two Notions of the Infinite," 71–86, available for download at http://richardghowe.com/index_htm_files/TwoNotionsoftheInfiniteinThomasAquinaslatest.pdf, accessed 06/20/23.

I know from experience that it can be convincing to some. But I also know that, having demonstrated that the universe had a beginning and, thus, needs a cause to account for its beginning, the argument says little about the nature of that cause.

To be sure, champions of the argument maintain that it shows that this cause must be timeless, spaceless, immaterial, inconceivably powerful, and personal. Interestingly, however, the kalam fails to show the one attribute of God that is most relevant in people's mind when it comes to the problem of evil, which is whether this cause is *good*. For most, including Whittenberger, something cannot be good in any relevant sense in which the problem of evil is concerned, without itself being moral. This is an important point of conflict in this conversation. Whittenberger maintains that God is conceived "as perfectly moral."[21] He challenges Huffling "to ask a random sample of people shopping at a public mall what they think on this issue" as he is "confident that most will see it as" he does.[22] I have no doubt Whittenberger is right. Even more, I suspect that if you took a sampling of contemporary Christian philosophers, you would get the same answer. But the question is not whether such a sampling might show that such a definition of God is held by the people at a mall or with Christian philosophers. Rather, the question is whether one *ought* to so define God as perfectly moral. It can be a tough subject of inquiry. I will not add my small contribution to what Huffling has already said beyond reminding Whittenberger that the definition of "moral" is impacted by whether or not one accepts the philosophical assumptions of classical theism as true. I fear that Whittenberger is taking "moral" according to the (as he calls it) modern definition when trying to evaluate Huffling's point that God is not a moral being.

In response to Huffling's appeal to such luminaries as Augustine, Anselm, and Aquinas, Whittenberger thinks it matters that Aquinas lived seven centuries ago; pointing out that it is too much to think that "we should expect the definitions of 'God' of these three men to measure up to the modern standard definition which I have presented."[23] A philosopher can only smile at such a suggestion. We can only hope that the time-honored Aristotelian "definition" of the law of non-contradiction can survive this test if we ask a random sample of mall shoppers about whether contradictory assertions can both be true at the same time and in the same respect,

---

21. *God, Evil, and Morality*, 55.
22. *God, Evil, and Morality*, 55.
23. *God, Evil, and Morality*, 56.

Part II: Commentaries on the Debate

especially in light of the fact that Aristotle lived nearly twenty-four centuries ago![24]

One attribute that Whittenberger left out of his list is aseity—God's self-existence. He left it out not because he denies that it is part of the "standard definition," but rather because he "did not think it was relevant to the particular arguments against God's existence on which we are focused."[25] This is an astounding admission. Whittenberger clearly does not see the connection between, on the one hand, why it is that God is self-existent and, on the other hand, how it is that God is good and how this answers the challenge of the problem of evil. It is little wonder why he does not appreciate exactly what Huffling all along has been trying to demonstrate. For whatever reason, one of Huffling's main points never got through to Whittenberger, much less was it ever refuted.

Granted, Whittenberger claims that Huffling "presented no arguments in this regard [that God is not moral] and so there are none to refute."[26] I am confident that all sides will admit that the constraints of the format of the conversion put important limits on how much each side could argue. Despite that constraint, Huffling does indeed give an argument involving his contrast between, on one hand, how human actions are connected to human flourishing (which is easily identifiable) which impacts our notion of human morality and, on the other hand, any coherent notion of God flourishing. If God is a perfect being, Huffling argues, then what could it even mean to say that one action or another will contribute to or subtract from God's flourishing? Perhaps one might think that Huffling has not said enough. As I suggested, all the interlocutors would likely say that no one said enough. Regardless, Huffling did give an argument in response to which Whittenberger had nothing to say. Again, I want to resist the temptation to insert myself too much into the debate. Perhaps I am too late for that. Suffice it to say that only when one understands how the flow of

---

24. Aristotle says, "But we have now posited that it is impossible for anything at the same time to be and not to be, and by this means have shown that this is the most indisputable of all principles. Some indeed demand that even this shall be demonstrated, but this they do through want of education, for not to know of what things one should demand demonstration, and of what one should not, argues want of education. For it is impossible that there should be demonstration of absolutely everything (there would be an infinite regress, so that there would still be no demonstration)." Aristotle, *The Basic Works of Aristotle*, 737.

25. *God, Evil, and Morality*, 56.

26. *God, Evil, and Morality*, 58.

Aquinas's argument of how "good" is convertible with "exist," will one be in a position to affirm or deny his conclusions that God exists, that God is good, and that God's goodness is demonstrable irrespective of whether there is evil in the world.[27]

Given that the debate here was designed to be conversational and not academic, it is understandable that the interlocutors did not engage the arguments at a more technical philosophical level. Though not surprising, it is regrettable (but the fault of no one here) that the philosophical assumptions that do come in to play from the critics, invariably arise from a modern and contemporary analytical philosophical perspective. The degree to which a reader might sense that the critics have made some inroads in showing how formidable a challenge the problem of evil is for the Christian only serves to reinforce in the mind of Christian Thomists—particularly existential Thomists as Huffling and I are—the shortcomings of modern and contemporary analytic philosophy in the relevant areas of the existence and nature of God and the nature of good and evil. It has been my experience that, not only with respect to the arguments with the atheists regarding God's existence, but also with respect to debates with certain Christian philosophers regarding the classical attributes of God, such arguments invariably come down to several foundational issues in metaphysics. To repeat a point I made at the beginning, Huffling did a herculean job of managing such a robust topic as the problem of evil within the constraints of such a conversational exchange.

---

27. For an exploration of Aquinas's thinking here, see Aertsen, "The Convertibility of Being," 449–70.

Bibliography

Adams, Marilyn McCord. *Horrendous Evils and the Goodness of God*. Ithaca, NY: Cornell University Press, 1999.
Aertsen, Jan A. "The Convertibility of Being and Good in St. Thomas Aquinas." *New Scholasticism* 59 (1985) 449–70.
Aquinas, Thomas. *On Being and Essence*. 2nd ed. Translated by Armand Maurer. Toronto: Pontifical Institute of Mediaeval Studies, 1968.
———. *Summa Contra Gentiles*. Translated by Vernon J. Bourke. Notre Dame, IN: University of Notre Dame Press, 1975.
———. *Summa Theologica*. Translated by the Fathers of English Dominican Province. London: Burns Oates & Washbourne, n.d.
Aristotle. *The Basic Works of Aristotle*. Edited by Richard McKeon. New York: Random House, 1941.
Augustine. *Confessions*. Translated by John K. Ryan. New York: Doubleday, 1960.
Augustyn, Adam. "Indian Ocean Tsunami of 2004." *Encyclopaedia Britannica*, 2019. https://bit.ly/2gyuBUo.
Benson, Herbert, et al. "Study of the Therapeutic Effects of Intercessory Prayer (STEP) in Cardiac Bypass Patients: A Multicenter Randomized Trial of Uncertainty and Certainty of Receiving Intercessory Prayer." *American Heart Journal* 151.4 (2006) 934–42.
Blackson, Thomas A. "Epicureanism." https://philarchive.org/archive/BLAE-10.
Boyd, Gregory A. *God of the Possible: A Biblical Introduction to the Open View of God*. Grand Rapids: Baker, 2000.
Carrier, Richard. "Is a Good God Logically Possible?" Blog. https://www.richardcarrier.info/archives/15794.
Copleston, Frederick. *A History of Philosophy, Vol. II: Augustine to Scotus*. Garden City, NY: Image, 1962.
Coté, Matthew J. "Truth's Light and Supereminent Darkness: The Problem of Univocal Concepts in Analogical Predication of God." PhD diss., Southern Evangelical Seminary, forthcoming.
Craig, William Lane. *The Kalām Cosmological Argument*. 1979. Reprint, Eugene, OR: Wipf and Stock, 2000.
———. *The Only Wise God: The Compatibility of Divine Foreknowledge and Human Freedom*. 1987. Reprint, Eugene, OR: Wipf and Stock, 2000.
Davies, Brian. *Introduction to the Philosophy of Religion*. 4th ed. Oxford: Oxford University Press, 2020.

Bibliography

———. *The Reality of God and the Problem of Evil*. London: Continuum, 2006.

Dolezal, James E. *All That Is in God: Evangelical Theology and the Challenge of Classical Christian Theism*. Grand Rapids: Reformation Heritage Books, 2017.

Geisler, Norman L. *Christian Apologetics*. 2nd ed. Grand Rapids: Baker Academic, 2013. Kindle.

———. *Systematic Theology, Vol. Two: God and Creation*. Minneapolis: Bethany House, 2003.

Grenz, Stanley, David Guretzki, and Cherith Fee Nordling. *Pocket Dictionary of Theological Terms*. Downers Grove, IL: InterVarsity, 1999.

Haines, David. *Natural Theology: A Biblical and Historical Introduction and Defense*. Leesburg, VA: Davenant, 2021.

Howard-Snyder, Daniel, ed. *The Evidential Argument from Evil*. Bloomington, IN: Indiana University Press, 1996. Kindle.

Howe, Richard G. "Two Notions of the Infinite in Thomas Aquinas' *Summa Theologiae* I, Questions 2 and 46." *Christian Apologetics Journal* 8.1 (2009) 71–86.

Huffling, J. Brian. "God Is Not a Moral Being: A Response to Gary Whittenberger on the Problem of Evil." *Skeptic* 24.4 (2019) 43–45.

———. "Is God Morally Obligated to Prevent Evil? A Response to James Sterba." *Religions* 12.5: 312 (2021). doi.org/10.3390/rel12050312.

———. "Is the Reality of Evil Good Evidence Against the Christian God? A Response to Michael Shermer's Affirmative Answer." *Skeptic* 24.2 (2019) 49–54.

———. "The Problem of Evil and God's Moral Standing: A Rejoinder to James Sterba." *Religions* 12.5: 312 (2022). doi.org/10.3390/rel13111031.

Hume, David. *Dialogues Concerning Natural Religion*. Amherst, MA: Prometheus, 1989.

Kenny, Anthony. *Studies in Ethics and the Philosophy of Religion*. Edited by D. Z. Phillips. Vol. V. *The Five Ways: St. Thomas Aquinas' Proofs of God's Existence*. 1969. Reprint, London: Routledge, 2003. Kindle.

Kerr, Gaven. *Aquinas's Way to God: The Proof in* De Ente et Essentia. Oxford: Oxford University Press, 2015.

Klubertanz, George P. *St. Thomas Aquinas on Analogy*. Chicago: Loyola University Press, 1960.

Knasas John F. X. *Thomistic Existentialism and Cosmological Reasoning*. Washington, DC: The Catholic University of America Press, 2019.

Kushner. Harold. *When Bad Things Happen to Good People*. Albany, NY: Anchor, 2004.

Leibniz, Gottfried Wilhelm. *Theodicy, Abridged*. Edited by Diogenes Allen. Indianapolis: Bobbs-Merrill, 1966.

Mackie, J. L. "Evil and Omnipotence." *Mind* 64.254 (1955) 200–201.

———. *The Miracle of Theism: Arguments for and Against the Existence of God*. Oxford: Clarendon, 1982.

Martin, Michael. *Atheism: A Philosophical Justification*. Philadelphia: Temple University Press, 1990.

McCabe, Herbert. *God and Evil: In the Theology of St. Thomas Aquinas*. New York: Continuum, 2010.

McInerny, Ralph. *Aquinas and Analogy*. Washington, DC: Catholic University of America, 1996.

Nash, Ronald H. *The Concept of God: An Exploration of Contemporary Difficulties with the Attributes of God*. Grand Rapids: Zondervan, 1983.

Bibliography

Owens, Joseph. *Cognition: An Epistemological Inquiry.* Houston: Center for Thomistic Studies, 1992.

Peterson, Michael L., ed. *The Problem of Evil: Selected Readings.* 2nd ed. Notre Dame, IN: Notre Dame Press, 2017. Kindle.

Plantinga, Alvin. *God, Freedom, and Evil.* Grand Rapids: Eerdmans, 1989.

Rocca, Gregory P. *Speaking the Incomprehensible God.* Washington, DC: The Catholic University of America Press, 2004.

Shermer, Michael. "Is the Reality of Evil Good Evidence Against the Christian God? Notes from a Debate on the Problem of Evil." *Skeptic* 24.2 (2019) 42–48.

———. *The Moral Arc: How Science Makes Us Better People.* New York: St. Martin's Griffin, 2015.

———. *The Science of Good and Evil: Why People Cheat, Gossip, Care, Share, and Follow the Golden Rule.* New York: Henry, Holt, and Company, 2004.

Steinhart Paul J., and Neil Turok. *Endless Universe: Beyond the Big Bang.* New York: Doubleday, 2007.

Stenger, Victor. *God, the Failed Hypothesis: How Science Shows That God Does Not Exist.* New York: Prometheus, 2007.

Sterba, James P. *Is a Good God Logically Possible?* London: Palgrave Macmillan, 2019.

———. "Sixteen Contributors: A Response." *Religions* 12.7: 536 (2021). doi.org/10.3390/rel12070536.

Tooley, Michael, "The Problem of Evil." In *The Stanford Encyclopedia of Philosophy* (Winter 2021), edited by Edward N. Zalta. plato.stanford.edu/archives/win2021/entries/evil/.

Weisberger, Andrea M. "The Argument from Evil." In *The Cambridge Companion to Atheism.* Edited by Michael Martin, 166–81. Cambridge: Cambridge University Press, 2007.

Whittenberger, Gary. "Does God Exist? A Rebuttal of Theologian Brian Huffling." *Skeptic* 24.4 (2019) 40–42.

———. *God Wants You to Be an Atheist: The Startling Conclusion from a Rational Analysis.* Denver: Outskirts, 2010.

Whittenberger, Gary J., and Nick Peters. *God and Natural Disasters: A Debate between an Atheist and a Christian.* Edited by J. P. Holding. No loc: Tektonic Plates, 2014. Kindle.

Wilhelmsen, Frederick D. *Man's Knowledge of Reality: An Introduction to Thomistic Epistemology.* Eaglewood Cliffs, NJ: Prentice-Hall, 1956.

Wykstra, Stephen. "A Skeptical Theist View." In *God and the Problem of Evil: Five Views.* Edited by Chad Meister and James K. Dew Jr., 99–100. Downers Grove, IL: IVP Academic, 2017.

www.ingramcontent.com/pod-product-compliance
Lightning Source LLC
Chambersburg PA
CBHW050818160426
43192CB00010B/1812